21ST CENTURY REVOLUTION

Guide for Personal and Professional Growth

ELIJAH CARTER

WSTech
Architects of Future

We find ourselves standing at the precipice of a new era—a digital frontier where the pursuit of personal development takes on a profoundly novel dimension. Welcome to a journey that transcends the ordinary bounds of self-improvement, where the boundless potential of artificial intelligence becomes a guiding force, illuminating the path towards a future that is not just brighter but teeming with prosperity and wisdom.

Elijah Carter

Contents

Your personal development journey using Artificial Intelligence

In a rapidly evolving world where technology continually extends its influence and moulds our daily experiences, we find ourselves on the brink of a new technological era. This digital frontier introduces a fresh perspective to personal development, inviting you to a journey beyond conventional self-improvement. Here, we leverage artificial intelligence's limitless potential to forge a future that is brighter and marked by prosperity and innovation.

The age-old pursuit of personal growth and financial prosperity has been, for generations, a noble endeavour pursued through sheer determination, grit, and human ingenuity. Yet, in this brave new world, a remarkable transformation is unfolding—one that promises to revolutionise how we approach our development and the pursuit of financial success.

In the following pages, we will embark on a captivating odyssey that explores the incredible synergy between personal development and AI-powered wealth generation. Together, we will navigate the intricate maze of possibilities, unveiling how AI can be harnessed not merely as a tool but as an ally that amplifies our potential, accelerates our progress, and empowers us to reach unprecedented heights.

As we delve into the heart of this journey, we will discover how AI, with its machine learning algorithms, natural language processing capabilities, and data-driven insights, can become a force multiplier for your personal and financial growth. It has the power to decipher your aspirations, streamline your efforts, and illuminate the path to prosperity with a precision that surpasses human capabilities alone.

We will explore how AI can craft compelling content, generate innovative business ideas, and facilitate monetisation strategies that were once considered beyond reach. You will gain a fresh perspective on entrepreneurship, investment, and wealth through AI.

Management—a perspective that transcends conventional wisdom and expands the horizons of what's possible.

But, as we embark on this extraordinary journey, let us remember that the true essence of personal development remains grounded in the human spirit. AI is a remarkable tool, but our aspirations, dreams, and determination infuse it with purpose and direction. This book is not just a manual on leveraging AI for financial gain; it's an invitation to rekindle your passion, set audacious goals, and use AI as your steadfast companion on the road to fulfilment and prosperity.

In the following pages, you will discover the stories of individuals who have harnessed the power of AI to transform their lives. Their experiences will serve as beacons of inspiration, guiding you towards your path of discovery and achievement.

So, dear reader, prepare to embark on a voyage that blends the profound wisdom of personal development with the cutting-edge marvels of AI. Together, we will unlock the boundless potential that resides within you and, in doing so, redefine what it means to achieve not just success but significance in the age of artificial intelligence.

ONE

The Origins

THE FASCINATION OF HUMANITY WITH intelligent machines has endured for centuries. However, the modern concept of artificial intelligence (AI) originated relatively recently, owing to the groundbreaking contributions of mathematicians, logicians, and computer scientists.

The fundamental objective of AI research is to emulate and replicate the computational processes of the human brain. In the 1940s, visionaries like Alan Turing laid the groundwork for AI by formulating conceptual frameworks to define this extraordinary field. Turing's renowned "Turing Test" proposed a method to determine if a machine could exhibit behaviour equivalent to human intelligence.

Fast forward to 1956, when the Dartmouth Conference marked a pivotal moment when AI research took flight.

Spearheaded by John McCarthy, Marvin Minsky, Nathaniel Rochester, and Claude Shannon, the conference not only coined the term "artificial intelligence" but also outlined an ambitious research agenda. Throughout the 1950s and 1960s, AI research focused on developing algorithms for general problem-solving to replicate the multifaceted nature of human cognition.

A significant breakthrough occurred in 1956 with the creation of the Logic Theorist programme by Allen Newell, Herbert Simon, and Cliff Shaw. This algorithm was capable of proving mathematical theorems and even discovering new proofs. However, it became evident that rule-based systems had limitations, as it was challenging to anticipate every conceivable scenario with predefined rules.

In the late 1950s, the tide shifted towards machine learning approaches. Arthur Samuel pioneered the development of programmes that could learn to play checkers through experience, signifying a significant turning point in AI research.

As the 1960s and 1970s unfolded, AI research diversified into specialised domains such as computer vision, speech recognition, and robotics. The advent of microelectronics revolutionised the development of practical AI systems. However, the 1970s witnessed a decline in funding for AI due to overpromising and underdelivering on the goal of simulating general human intelligence. This period, known as the "AI winter," persisted until the 1980s.

The 1980s saw a resurgence in AI research with the emergence of expert systems. These knowledge-based programmes encoded domain expertise and empowered AI to solve problems in specialised fields like medical diagnosis. However, the construction and maintenance of rule-based systems proved prohibitively expensive.

A paradigm shift occurred with the rise of machine learning and neural networks. Inspired by the neural circuitry of the human brain, neural networks are computational models capable of discerning patterns from training data without relying on predefined rules. The backpropagation algorithm, developed in the 1970s, facilitated efficient training of multi-layer neural networks.

From the 1990s onwards, breakthroughs in machine learning accelerated the capabilities of AI. The exponential data availability and computing power growth fueled rapid advancements in statistical and deep learning techniques. Applications such as computer vision, speech recognition, and machine translation have reached unprecedented levels of capability and accuracy, and the 21st century witnessed the emergence of digital assistants, recommendation engines, and more, making AI ubiquitous daily.

The recent explosion of AI has yielded remarkable achievements, from self-driving cars to AI-generated multimedia content. Programmes have even mastered complex games like chess and go through self-play. However, the ultimate goal of AI, artificial general intelligence (AGI)—AI with the multidimensional capabilities of human cognition—remains elusive. The quest to create genuinely intelligent machines persists, and with responsible stewardship, AI has the potential to forge a prosperous and equitable future for all.

TWO

Understanding the benefits

ENHANCING PRODUCTIVITY AND EFFICIENCY through automation is a paramount objective for businesses in various industries. By harnessing the power of technology and innovative tools, organisations can streamline their operations, reduce manual tasks, and achieve heightened output levels.

Automation presents a multitude of advantages for enterprises. One key benefit is the potential to enhance accuracy and diminish errors. Manual processes are susceptible to human error, leading to costly mistakes and delays. Businesses can automate repetitive tasks to minimise the risk of errors and ensure consistent and reliable results.

Additionally, automation reduces errors and enables increased speed and efficiency. Automated systems can perform tasks much faster than humans, empowering organisations to complete work more expeditiously and meet deadlines more effectively. This heightened efficiency saves time and allows employees to concentrate on more strategic and value-added endeavours.

Another advantage of automation is the capacity to scale operations without significant cost escalation. As businesses expand and demand intensifies, manual processes may become overwhelmed and incapable of keeping up. Automation provides a scalable solution, enabling companies to handle higher work volumes without necessitating additional resources. This scalability is crucial in fast-paced industries where agility and responsiveness are vital for success.

Furthermore, automation can enhance collaboration and communication within an organisation. By automating workflows and processes, teams can effortlessly share information and collaborate. This streamlined collaboration improves productivity and ensures everyone is aligned, leading to better decision-making and outcomes.

Implementing automation necessitates meticulous planning and consideration. It is imperative to evaluate which processes are suitable for automation and ensure the necessary infrastructure and resources are available. Additionally, organisations should provide adequate training and support to employees to ensure a smooth transition to automated systems.

Enhancing productivity and efficiency through automation is a strategic imperative for businesses. By leveraging technology and automation tools, companies can optimise their operations, minimise errors, increase speed and scalability, and foster collaboration. Embracing automation improves the bottom line and empowers employees to focus on more meaningful and creative work. As technology evolves, embracing automation will be essential for organisations to stay competitive and thrive in the digital age.

Streamlining decision-making processes can significantly enhance organisational efficiency and effectiveness. By implementing streamlined approaches, businesses can minimise delays and bottlenecks, leading to quicker and more informed decisions. This, in turn, can improve overall productivity and performance.

One key aspect of streamlining decision-making processes is eliminating unnecessary steps and complexities. Simplifying decision-making frameworks and removing redundant layers of approval can expedite the process and empower employees to make decisions more autonomously. This saves time and promotes a culture of agility and innovation within the organisation.

Another important factor in streamlining decision-making is the effective use of technology and automation. Leveraging digital tools and platforms can enable real-time data collection, analysis, and visualisation, providing decision-makers with accurate and up-to-date information. This enables faster and more precise decision-making and the ability to track and evaluate the impact of decisions over time.

Furthermore, fostering a collaborative decision-making culture can also contribute to streamlining processes. By involving relevant stakeholders and seeking input from diverse perspectives, organisations can ensure that decisions are well-informed and consider a wide range of considerations. This collaborative approach helps generate better solutions and increases buy-in and commitment from those affected by the decisions.

Additionally, establishing clear decision-making frameworks and guidelines can streamline the process by providing a structured approach for evaluating options and making choices. Organisations can avoid unnecessary delays and confusion by defining criteria, setting priorities, and establishing decision-making roles and responsibilities. This clarity enables faster and more efficient decision-making while still ensuring that decisions are well-considered and aligned with organisational goals.

Streamlining decision-making processes is crucial for organisations seeking to improve efficiency and effectiveness. Businesses can make decisions faster, more accurately, and with more significant impact by simplifying processes, leveraging technology, fostering collaboration, and establishing improvements. Ultimately, this can lead to improved performance, agility, and competitive advantage in today's fast-paced and ever-changing business landscape.

Improving customer experiences through personalisation is a pivotal aspect of modern business. By tailoring products, services, and interactions to meet the unique needs and preferences of individual customers, companies can create more meaningful and valuable experiences. Personalisation allows businesses to build stronger customer relationships, increase customer satisfaction and loyalty, and ultimately drive business growth.

One of the critical benefits of personalisation is the ability to deliver relevant and timely content to customers. By collecting and analysing customer data, businesses can gain insights into customer behaviours, preferences, and purchase stories. This data can then segment customers into different groups based on their characteristics and preferences. With this information, businesses can create targeted marketing campaigns, recommend personalised product offerings, and provide relevant content that resonates with each customer segment.

Personalisation also enables businesses to provide a more seamless and convenient customer experience. Companies can create personalised user interfaces by leveraging customer data, optimising website navigation, and streamlining purchasing. For example, an e-commerce website can use personalisation to display product recommendations based on a customer's browsing history or previous purchases. This enhances the customer's shopping experience and increases the likelihood of a successful sale.

Furthermore, personalisation can help businesses build stronger relationships with their customers. Companies can tailor their communications and interactions to be more relevant and meaningful by understanding customer preferences and needs.

For instance, a personalised email that addresses a customer by name and offers recommendations based on their previous purchases will likely resonate more with the customer than a generic email blast. This personalised approach shows customers that the business values their individuality and is invested in their satisfaction.

In addition to improving customer experiences, personalisation can lead to increased customer satisfaction and loyalty. When customers feel understood and valued by a business, they are more likely to become repeat customers and advocates for the brand. By consistently delivering personalised experiences, companies can foster customer loyalty and generate positive word-of-mouth recommendations. This, in turn, can attract new customers and contribute to business growth.

Implementing personalisation strategies requires combining technology, data analysis, and a customer-centric mindset. Businesses must invest in robust customer relationship management (CRM) systems, data analytics tools, and automation technologies to effectively collect, analyse, and leverage customer data. They also need to prioritise customer privacy and data protection to ensure that personalisation efforts are carried out ethically and in compliance with relevant regulations.

Personalisation plays a crucial role in improving customer experiences. By tailoring products, services, and interactions to meet individual customer needs, businesses can create more meaningful and valuable experiences. Personalisation not only enhances customer satisfaction and loyalty but also drives business growth. As technology advances and customer expectations evolve, businesses prioritising personalisation will be better positioned to succeed in the increasingly competitive marketplace.

Revolutionising healthcare, education, and other sectors has been a transformative force in society. The advancements in these fields have profoundly impacted how we live, learn, and receive medical care. In the realm of healthcare, revolutionary technologies and treatments have emerged, improving patient outcomes and transforming the delivery of care. From the development of life-saving medications to the use of telemedicine, access to quality healthcare has become more widespread and convenient. These innovations have bridged the gap between patients and healthcare providers, enabling remote consultations and personalised treatment plans.

Education has also revolutionised, with technological advancements and teaching methods reshaping the learning experience. Online education platforms have made learning more accessible and flexible, allowing individuals to pursue knowledge at their own pace and from anywhere in the world. Interactive digital tools and virtual reality simulations have enhanced the engagement and understanding of complex subjects, revolutionising how knowledge is acquired and shared.

Furthermore, the impact of these revolutions extends beyond healthcare and education. Various sectors, such as transportation, communication, and entertainment, have been revolutionised through technological breakthroughs. The advent of electric vehicles and autonomous driving has transformed how we commute, reducing our carbon footprint and improving road safety. Communication has been revolutionised with the rise of social media platforms and instant messaging apps, enabling real-time global connectivity and facilitating the exchange of ideas. The entertainment industry has been revolutionised by streaming services, allowing us to access a vast array of content anytime, anywhere.

In conclusion, revolutionising healthcare, education, and other sectors has brought significant advancements and positive societal changes. These innovations have improved access, efficiency, and outcomes, making our lives easier, more connected, and more productive. As we embrace and adapt to these revolutions, we can look forward to a future filled with endless possibilities and continued progress.

THREE

Business

USING ARTIFICIAL INTELLIGENCE (AI) IN DATA analysis and predictive modelling has brought about a revolutionary shift in the decision-making processes of businesses and organisations. By utilising advanced algorithms and machine learning techniques, AI enables the extraction of valuable insights from vast and complex datasets, thereby empowering companies to gain a competitive advantage in today's data-driven world.

One of the primary benefits of employing AI in data analysis is its ability to process large amounts of information in a fraction of the time it would take humans to perform the same task. Traditional data analysis methods often require manual sorting, filtering, and aggregation, which consume time and are prone to errors. In contrast, AI algorithms effortlessly handle massive datasets, quickly identifying patterns, correlations, and trends that may not be immediately apparent to human analysts.

Predictive modelling, another critical application of AI in data analysis, enables businesses to forecast future outcomes based on historical data. Organisations can make accurate predictions about future events or trends by training AI models on past observations and their corresponding outcomes. This predictive capability holds immense value across various domains, including finance, healthcare, marketing, and supply chain management. For example, financial institutions can utilise AI-powered predictive models to assess credit risk, identify fraud patterns, and optimise investment strategies.

Furthermore, AI-driven data analysis can uncover hidden insights and better understand complex phenomena. Traditional statistical methods may overlook subtle relationships or nonlinear patterns in the data, whereas AI algorithms excel at discovering intricate connections that may not be immediately apparent. This enhanced understanding opens new avenues for innovation, enabling businesses to find new market opportunities, improve customer experiences, and optimise operational processes.

However, it is essential to acknowledge that using AI in data analysis also presents challenges and considerations. The quality and reliability of the data used to train AI models are paramount. Biases or inaccuracies in the training data can lead to biased or misleading results. Therefore, ensuring that the data used for analysis is representative, diverse, and free from any systematic errors or biases is crucial.

Furthermore, the interpretability of AI models is another aspect that requires attention. While AI algorithms can provide accurate predictions, understanding the underlying reasons for these predictions can be a complex task. This lack of interpretability can limit the trust and acceptance of AI-driven insights, especially in domains where explainability and transparency are crucial, such as healthcare or legal decision-making.

Using AI in data analysis and predictive modelling has transformed how organisations extract insights and make informed decisions. By leveraging its speed, scalability, and ability to uncover hidden patterns, AI empowers businesses to gain a competitive advantage in today's data-driven landscape. However, it is essential to address challenges such as data quality and interpretability to ensure AI's ethical and responsible use in data analysis. Integrating AI into data analysis has revolutionised decision-making processes for businesses and organisations.

FOUR

Everyday Life

Smart homes and Internet of Things (IoT) applications have revolutionised how we live and interact with our surroundings. With the advancement of technology, our homes have become more intelligent and connected than ever before. From controlling our lights and appliances with a simple voice command to monitoring our security systems remotely, smart homes offer convenience, comfort, and increased energy efficiency.

The Internet of Things (IoT) has played a significant role in developing smart homes. It refers to the network of interconnected devices, sensors, and systems that communicate with each other to collect and exchange data. These devices range from everyday household items like thermostats, refrigerators, and door locks to wearable devices and cars. The data collected by these devices can be analysed and used to automate tasks, improve efficiency, and enhance the overall living experience.

One of the key benefits of smart homes and IoT applications is the ability to remotely control and monitor various aspects of our homes. With the help of smartphone apps or voice assistants, homeowners can adjust the temperature, turn on and off lights, lock doors, and even monitor their home security cameras from anywhere in the world. This level of control and convenience saves time and provides peace of mind.

Energy efficiency is another significant advantage of smart homes and IoT applications. With smart thermostats and energy monitoring devices, homeowners can optimise their energy usage and reduce their carbon footprint. These devices can analyse energy consumption patterns and adjust accordingly, ensuring that energy is used efficiently and waste minimised. This helps save money on utility bills and contributes to a greener and more sustainable future.

Furthermore, smart homes and IoT applications can potentially improve safety and security. Connected devices like smart locks, doorbell cameras, and motion sensors can provide real-time alerts and notifications, allowing homeowners to monitor and protect their properties effectively. In addition, intelligent smoke detectors and water leak sensors can detect potential hazards and send immediate messages, helping to prevent accidents and minimise damage.

However, as with any technology, there are challenges and considerations regarding smart homes and IoT applications. Privacy and data security are significant concerns, as these devices collect and transmit personal information. Homeowners must ensure their smart home systems are secure and protected from unauthorised access. Regular software updates, strong passwords, and encryption are some of the measures that can help mitigate these risks.

Smart homes and Internet of Things (IoT) applications have completely transformed our way of life and our interaction with the environment. Technological advancements have made our homes more intelligent and interconnected than ever. They now offer unparalleled convenience, comfort, and enhanced energy efficiency.

The Internet of Things (IoT) has played a pivotal role in the evolution of smart homes. It encompasses a network of interconnected devices, sensors, and systems that communicate with one another to gather and exchange data. These devices span everyday household items like thermostats, refrigerators, and door locks to wearable devices and even automobiles. The data collected by these devices can be analysed and utilised to automate tasks, optimise efficiency, and enrich the overall living experience.

One of the notable advantages of smart homes and IoT applications is the ability to control and monitor various aspects of our homes remotely. Through smartphone applications or voice-activated assistants, homeowners can effortlessly adjust temperature settings, activate or deactivate lights, secure doors, and even watch their home security cameras from anywhere around the globe. This level of control and convenience saves time and instils a sense of tranquillity.

Energy efficiency is another significant benefit derived from smart homes and IoT applications. Smart thermostats and energy monitoring devices enable homeowners to optimise their energy consumption and reduce their carbon footprint. These devices analyse energy usage patterns and make necessary adjustments to ensure efficient utilisation and minimise waste. This translates into cost savings on utility bills and contributes to a more eco-friendly and sustainable future.

Furthermore, smart homes and IoT applications possess significant potential for enhancing safety and security. Connected devices, such as smart locks, doorbell cameras, and motion sensors, provide real-time alerts and notifications, enabling homeowners to monitor and safeguard their properties effectively. Additionally, intelligent smoke detectors and water leak sensors promptly detect potential hazards and issue immediate notifications, thereby preventing accidents and minimising damage. However, like any technological innovation, smart homes and IoT applications also present challenges and considerations. Privacy and data security are significant concerns, as these devices collect and transmit personal information. Homeowners must ensure the security and protection of their smart home systems against unauthorised access. Implementing regular software updates, employing solid passwords, and utilising encryption are among the measures that can help mitigate these risks.

One area where AI has made significant strides in recent years is healthcare. With the ability to analyse vast amounts of medical data and assist in diagnosis, AI has the potential to revolutionise healthcare delivery. For instance, AI-powered chatbots can provide immediate assistance and triage patients based on their symptoms, potentially saving patients and healthcare providers valuable time. Moreover, AI-driven imaging tools can aid in the early detection of diseases like cancer, allowing for earlier intervention and potentially better patient outcomes. AI algorithms can analyse medical images with accuracy that surpasses human capabilities, making them valuable tools in the fight against diseases.

The advent of smart homes and the Internet of Things (IoT) has transformed our lifestyle and how we interact with our surroundings. Technological advancements have made our homes more intelligent and interconnected, offering unparalleled convenience, comfort, and energy efficiency.

The Internet of Things (IoT) has played a crucial role in the evolution of smart homes, encompassing a network of interconnected devices, sensors, and systems that communicate to gather and exchange data. These devices range from everyday household items like thermostats, refrigerators, and door locks to wearable devices and even automobiles. The data collected by these devices can be analysed and utilised to automate tasks, optimise efficiency, and enhance the overall living experience.

One of the notable advantages of smart homes and IoT applications is the ability to control and monitor various aspects of our homes remotely. Through smartphone applications or voice-activated assistants, homeowners can effortlessly adjust temperature settings, activate or deactivate lights, secure doors, and even watch their home security cameras from anywhere in the world. This level of control and convenience saves time and instils a sense of tranquillity.

Energy efficiency is another significant benefit derived from smart homes and IoT applications. Smart thermostats and energy monitoring devices enable homeowners to optimise their energy consumption and reduce their carbon footprint. These devices analyse energy usage patterns and make necessary adjustments to ensure efficient utilisation and minimise waste. This translates into cost savings on utility bills and contributes to a more eco-friendly and sustainable future.

Furthermore, smart homes and IoT applications possess significant potential for enhancing safety and security. Connected devices, such as smart locks, doorbell cameras, and motion sensors, provide real-time alerts and notifications, enabling homeowners to monitor and safeguard their properties effectively. Additionally, intelligent smoke detectors and water leak sensors promptly detect potential hazards and issue immediate notifications, thereby preventing accidents and minimising damage. However, like any technological innovation, smart homes and IoT applications also present challenges and considerations. Privacy and data security are significant concerns, as these devices collect and transmit personal information. Home-owners must ensure the security and protection of their smart home systems against unauthorised access. Implementing regular software updates, employing solid passwords, and utilising encryption are among the measures that can help mitigate these risks.

Smart homes and Internet of Things (IoT) applications have completely transformed our way of life and our interaction with the environment. Technological advancements have made our homes more intelligent and interconnected than ever. They now offer unparalleled convenience, comfort, and enhanced energy efficiency, contributing to a more environmentally friendly and sustainable future.

Smart homes and IoT applications offer numerous advantages, including enhanced energy efficiency. Homeowners can optimise their energy consumption and decrease carbon emissions using smart thermostats and monitoring devices. These devices analyse energy usage patterns and make necessary adjustments to ensure efficient utilisation and minimise waste. As a result, homes experience cost savings on utility bills and contribute to a more eco-friendly and sustainable future. Additionally, smart homes and IoT applications have the potential to improve safety and security significantly. Connected devices such as smart locks, doorbell cameras, and motion sensors provide real-time alerts and notifications, enabling homeowners to monitor and protect their properties effectively.

Smart smoke detectors and water leak sensors promptly detect potential hazards and issue immediate notifications, preventing accidents and minimising damage. However, it is essential to acknowledge the challenges and considerations associated with smart homes and IoT applications. Privacy and data security are significant concerns, as these devices collect and transmit personal information. Homeowners must prioritise the security and protection of their smart home systems against unauthorised access. Implementing regular software updates, strong passwords, and encryption are essential to mitigate these risks.

Let us not forget that at the core of all technological advancements is the desire to improve our lives and make things easier. As we continue to innovate and integrate technology into various aspects of our lives, let us never lose sight of this goal. Let us strive to use technology to promote progress and well-being for all individuals and society.

Technology has undoubtedly changed the world in ways we could have never imagined. It has opened up new possibilities and opportunities while presenting challenges that we must navigate responsibly.

AI in transportation and autonomous vehicles have revolutionised how we commute and travel. With advancements in artificial intelligence, the transportation industry has witnessed significant transformations, paving the way for safer, more efficient, and more sustainable modes of transportation.

Autonomous vehicles, commonly known as self-driving cars, are a prime example of the integration of AI technology in transportation. These vehicles are equipped with sophisticated sensors, cameras, and AI algorithms that enable them to perceive their surroundings, make decisions, and navigate without human intervention. The implementation of autonomous vehicles has the potential to enhance road safety by minimising human errors, which are often the cause of accidents.

In addition to safety, AI technology in transportation also brings about efficiency improvements. AI algorithms can analyse vast amounts of data in real-time, optimising routes and reducing traffic congestion. This saves commuters time and reduces fuel consumption and carbon emissions, contributing to a greener and more sustainable transportation system.

The use of AI extends beyond autonomous vehicles. AI-powered systems are being deployed in various aspects of transportation, such as traffic management, predictive maintenance, and logistics. Traffic management systems utilise AI algorithms to monitor and analyse traffic patterns, enabling authorities to make informed decisions to alleviate congestion and improve overall traffic flow.

Predictive maintenance is another area where AI is making a significant impact. By analysing data collected from sensors and monitoring equipment, AI algorithms can detect potential faults or performance issues in vehicles or infrastructure before they occur. This proactive approach to maintenance helps prevent breakdowns and reduces downtime, ensuring more reliable and efficient transportation services.

AI is revolutionising the logistics industry. Through intelligent optimisation algorithms, AI systems can optimise the planning and scheduling of transportation routes, minimising costs and maximising efficiency. These systems can also provide real-time tracking and monitoring of shipments, enhancing transparency and improving customer satisfaction.

While AI in transportation offers numerous benefits, it also presents challenges that must be addressed. AI systems' safety and security are paramount, as any vulnerabilities or malfunctions could have severe consequences. The ethical considerations surrounding AI decision-making in critical situations must be carefully examined and regulated.

AI in transportation and autonomous vehicles can transform how we travel and commute. From autonomous cars to traffic management systems and logistics optimisation, AI technology is revolutionising the transportation industry by enhancing safety, efficiency, and sustainability. However, addressing the challenges associated with AI implementation is crucial to ensure this technology's responsible and beneficial use in transportation.

AI in entertainment and gaming has revolutionised how we experience and interact with various forms of media. From movies and music to video games and virtual reality, artificial intelligence has become an integral part of the entertainment industry, enhancing our entertainment experiences in numerous ways.

One area where AI has made significant advancements is in the creation and production of content. With the help of AI algorithms, content creators can now generate realistic characters, immersive environments, and captivating storylines. By analysing vast amounts of data and learning from patterns, AI algorithms can develop creative and unique content that resonates with audiences.

AI has been employed in various aspects of film and television, including scriptwriting, video editing, and visual effects. AI algorithms can analyse scripts and generate scene suggestions, helping filmmakers streamline the creative process. AI-powered video editing tools can also automate tasks like colour correction and scene transitions, saving time and effort.

In music, AI has facilitated the exploration of new sounds and genres. AI algorithms can analyse vast music libraries and identify patterns and similarities, enabling musicians to experiment with different styles and create innovative compositions. Moreover, AI-powered virtual musicians and DJs have emerged, capable of composing and performing music indistinguishable from human-created music.

The gaming industry has also embraced AI-enhanced gameplay and created more immersive experiences. AI-powered game characters can exhibit human-like behaviour, adapting to player actions and making the gaming experience more challenging and engaging. Additionally, AI algorithms can analyse player behaviour and preferences, providing personalised recommendations for game content, difficulty levels, and in-game purchases.

The advancements in artificial intelligence (AI) have also had a positive impact on virtual reality (VR) and augmented reality (AR). Using AI algorithms, real-time sensor data can be analysed, and virtual environments can be adjusted accordingly, resulting in more immersive and lifelike VR experiences. Additionally, AI-powered AR applications can identify and track objects in real-time, seamlessly integrating virtual content into the physical world.

While AI has brought significant advantages to the entertainment and gaming industries, it also presents challenges and ethical considerations. Privacy concerns, algorithmic biases, and the potential impact on employment must be carefully addressed as AI advances in these domains.

In conclusion, AI has revolutionised the entertainment and gaming industries, offering new possibilities and enhancing the overall experience for audiences. From creating content to gameplay, AI has fundamentally transformed how we engage with and consume entertainment media. As AI continues to evolve, it will undoubtedly shape the future of entertainment and gaming, pushing boundaries and unlocking new creative opportunities.

FIVE

Personal Development

AI-BASED LEARNING PLATFORMS AND personalised education have revolutionised knowledge acquisition thanks to advancements in artificial intelligence. These platforms provide tailored learning experiences that cater to individual learners' unique needs and preferences. By leveraging AI algorithms, these platforms can analyse user data, identify patterns, and adapt the learning content accordingly.

One of the critical advantages of AI-based learning platforms is their ability to offer personalised recommendations and content. Unlike traditional educational methods that follow a one-size-fits-all approach, AI-based platforms consider various factors, such as learning style, proficiency level, and interests, to deliver customised content. This personalised approach enhances engagement and motivation, as learners are likelier to be invested in materials relevant to their specific goals and interests.

Furthermore, AI-based learning platforms can provide real-time feedback and assessments. Using machine learning algorithms, these platforms can analyse learners' performance, identify areas for improvement, and provide targeted feedback. This immediate feedback loop lets learners track their progress and adjust their learning strategies. Additionally, AI algorithms can adapt the difficulty level of the content based on learners' performance, ensuring that they are consistently challenged without feeling overwhelmed.

Another advantage of AI-based learning platforms is their ability to facilitate collaborative learning experiences. Intelligent algorithms connect learners with similar interests or complementary skill sets, fostering peer-to-peer interactions and knowledge sharing. Collaborative learning enhances understanding, retention, critical thinking, and problem-solving skills.

Moreover, AI-based platforms can leverage big data and analytics to gather insights about learners' behaviours and preferences. Educators and content creators can analyse this data to gain valuable insights into the effectiveness of different teaching methods and strategies. This data-driven approach enables continuous improvement and optimisation of learning materials and methodologies, ensuring learners receive the most effective and relevant content.

AI-based learning platforms and personalised education have transformed the educational landscape. By harnessing the power of artificial intelligence, these platforms offer tailored learning experiences, personalised recommendations, real-time feedback, collaborative learning opportunities, and data-driven insights. As technology advances, AI-based learning platforms will play an increasingly crucial role in shaping the future of education, empowering learners to achieve their full potential.

AI-driven fitness and health tracking have revolutionised approaches to well-being, thanks to advancements in artificial intelligence technology. Individuals now have access to innovative tools and applications that can help them monitor and improve their physical fitness and overall health.

One of the critical benefits of AI-driven fitness and health tracking is its ability to provide personalised insights and recommendations. By analysing data from wearable devices, mobile apps, and online platforms, AI algorithms can generate comprehensive reports on fitness levels, sleep patterns, nutrition, and other health metrics. These insights allow individuals to understand their bodies better and make informed decisions to optimise their well-being.

Furthermore, AI-driven fitness and health tracking can enhance workout routines. By leveraging machine learning algorithms, these tools can analyse exercise patterns, provide real-time feedback on form and technique, and suggest personalised workout plans. This helps individuals stay motivated and exercise safely and effectively to achieve their fitness goals.

In addition to fitness tracking, AI technology can play a significant role in monitoring health conditions. For individuals with chronic diseases or specific health concerns, AI-driven health tracking systems can provide continuous monitoring, alerting individuals to deviations from the norm. These systems can detect early warning signs, allowing individuals to take proactive measures and seek medical attention when necessary.

Moreover, AI-driven fitness and health tracking can foster a sense of community and support. Many platforms offer social features that allow users to connect with like-minded individuals, share progress, and engage in friendly competitions. This social aspect adds an element of fun to the fitness journey and provides a support system that helps individuals stay motivated and accountable.

However, it is essential to recognise that AI-driven fitness and health tracking pose challenges and considerations. Privacy and data security are critical concerns, as these platforms collect and analyse sensitive personal information. Users need to understand how their data is used and ensure that appropriate safeguards are in place to protect their privacy.

AI-driven fitness and health tracking can revolutionise approaches to physical well-being. By leveraging the power of artificial intelligence, individuals can gain valuable insights, improve workout routines, monitor health conditions, and connect with a supportive community. However, balancing the benefits with privacy and data security considerations is crucial. With responsible use and continuous advancements in AI technology, individuals can harness the full potential of AI-driven fitness and health tracking to lead healthier and more fulfilling lives.

AI has become increasingly prevalent in personal finance and investment management. With technological advancements, individuals can now access sophisticated tools and platforms to help them make informed financial decisions and optimise their investment portfolios.

One area where AI has significantly impacted is personal budgeting and expense tracking. Traditional methods often involve manual data entry and calculations, which can be time-consuming and error-prone. AI-powered personal finance apps and platforms automate these processes, making it easier for individuals to set budgets, track spending, and identify areas for saving money. These tools also provide personalised recommendations and insights based on an individual's financial goals and spending habits.

When it comes to investment management, AI has revolutionised the way portfolios are managed and optimised. AI algorithms can analyse vast amounts of data, such as market trends, historical performance, and individual investor preferences, to identify investment opportunities and generate personalised investment strategies. These algorithms can also continuously monitor and adjust portfolios based on changing market conditions, ensuring that investments align with an individual's goals and risk tolerance.

AI-powered investment platforms offer benefits such as automated portfolio rebalancing, tax optimisation, and access to alternative investment options. These platforms aim to democratise investment management, making it accessible to a broader range of individuals and helping them achieve their financial goals.

However, it is essential to note that while AI can provide valuable insights and recommendations, it should not replace human judgment and decision-making. The role of AI in personal finance and investment management is to augment and support individuals in their decision-making processes rather than replace their expertise.

AI has transformed personal finance and investment management by providing individuals with powerful tools and platforms to make informed financial decisions and optimise their investment portfolios. From budgeting and expense tracking to portfolio management and optimisation, AI has made these processes more efficient and accessible. By leveraging AI technology, individuals can take control of their finances and work towards achieving their financial goals.

AI has made remarkable strides in various fields, including creativity and artistic expression. With the ability to analyse massive amounts of data and learn from patterns, AI has opened new possibilities for artists, musicians, writers, and other creative individuals.

One area where AI has made significant contributions is in generating artistic content. AI algorithms can analyse vast collections of artwork, music, or literature and develop new pieces that mimic the style or characteristics of renowned artists. This has sparked debates about the nature of creativity and the role of AI in the artistic process. Some argue that AI-generated art lacks human touch and emotional depth, while others see it as a tool for inspiration and collaboration.

AI has also revolutionised the way artists create and experiment with new ideas. Through machine learning algorithms, AI can analyse patterns and generate suggestions or variations based on artists' existing work. This process can help artists explore new directions, break creative blocks, and discover unexpected possibilities. By augmenting human creativity, AI has become a valuable tool for artists to expand their horizons.

It has played a significant role in enhancing the accessibility of art and creativity. AI-powered platforms and applications allow individuals with limited artistic skills or physical abilities to engage in creative activities. For example, AI-based drawing tools can assist users in creating digital artwork by providing real-time feedback and suggestions. This democratisation of creativity has empowered people from diverse backgrounds to express themselves artistically.

However, creativity also raises ethical and legal concerns. Questions about copyright, ownership, and originality arise as AI advances. Who owns AI-generated artwork or music? Can AI infringe on copyrighted material? These questions challenge traditional notions of authorship and intellectual property rights, requiring new legal frameworks and ethical considerations.

There are concerns about AI replacing human artists and creative professionals. While AI can assist in generating ideas and content, the human element of artistry, emotion, and interpretation is irreplaceable. Artists bring unique perspectives and experiences that shape their work, and AI should be seen as a complementary tool rather than a substitute.

Looking ahead, the future of AI in creativity and artistic expression is promising yet uncertain. As AI technologies evolve, they will undoubtedly profoundly impact the creative process. However, it is essential to strike a balance between the capabilities of AI and the human touch in art. By embracing AI as a tool for inspiration, collaboration, and accessibility, we can unlock new dimensions of creativity and push the boundaries of artistic expression.

AI has emerged as a powerful force in creativity and artistic expression. From generating art to assisting artists and enhancing accessibility, AI has transformed the creative landscape. However, ethical and legal considerations and preserving human artistry should be at the forefront of this evolving relationship between AI and creativity. By embracing AI as a partner, artists and creators can embrace new opportunities and push the boundaries of their imagination.

SIX

Ethical Considerations

Privacy concerns and data security are paramount in the current digital era. With the growing dependence on technology and the extensive sharing of personal information online, addressing these concerns and safeguarding sensitive data is more crucial than ever.

One of the primary concerns regarding privacy is the collection and utilisation of personal information by companies and organisations. In many instances, individuals may not be fully aware of the extent to which their data is being collected and how it is being utilised. This lack of transparency can result in losing control over personal information and raise apprehension about potential misuse.

Data security is another significant facet of the privacy discourse. With the persistent threat of cyberattacks and data breaches, ensuring the security of personal information has become a top priority. Organisations must implement robust security measures to protect sensitive data from unauthorised access, loss, or theft. This includes the implementation of encryption, firewalls, and other security protocols to safeguard personal information.

Moreover, internal data breaches can also occur, posing risks to privacy. Employees with access to sensitive information may intentionally or unintentionally misuse or mishandle data, leading to potential privacy breaches. Organisations must establish strict access controls and provide comprehensive training to employees to mitigate these risks.

To address these concerns, governments and regulatory bodies have enacted various laws and regulations to protect privacy and ensure data security. For instance, the General Data Protection Regulation (GDPR) of the European Union establishes stringent guidelines for the collection, use, and processing of personal data. This includes the requirement for organisations to obtain explicit consent from individuals before collecting their data and granting individuals the right to access, correct, or delete their personal information.

Individuals are also responsible for protecting their privacy and data security. Individuals can mitigate the risk of privacy breaches by being mindful of the information they share online and taking steps to secure their devices and accounts. This involves using strong, unique passwords, enabling two-factor authentication, and exercising caution when sharing personal information on social media platforms.

Privacy concerns and data security require ongoing attention and action. Organisations must prioritise protecting personal information and implement robust security measures to mitigate the risks of privacy and data breaches. Governments and regulatory bodies are pivotal in setting guidelines and enforcing regulations to safeguard privacy rights. Ultimately, individuals also have a responsibility to take steps to protect their own privacy and data security in an increasingly digital world.

The impact of AI algorithms on bias and fairness has emerged as a significant subject of discussion and debate in recent years. As artificial intelligence continues to play a prominent role in various aspects of our lives, it is essential to examine the potential biases present in these algorithms and ensure fairness in their outcomes.

AI algorithms are designed to learn from data and make predictions or decisions based on that information. However, societal biases or historical disparities can influence the data used to train these algorithms. This can result in biased outcomes that disproportionately affect certain groups or perpetuate existing inequalities.

One area that has received considerable attention regarding bias in AI algorithms is the criminal justice system. Predictive policing algorithms, for example, are employed to identify areas with a high likelihood of crime. However, if the training data used to develop these algorithms is biased towards specific neighbourhoods or demographics, it can lead to over-policing in those communities and perpetuate systemic biases.

Similarly, AI algorithms used in hiring processes can inadvertently introduce bias and discrimination. If the training data used to develop these algorithms reflects biases in previous hiring decisions, it can perpetuate discriminatory practices and hinder efforts towards diversity and inclusion. It is crucial to critically evaluate and address these biases to ensure fair and equitable hiring practices.

Addressing bias and promoting fairness in AI algorithms is a complex undertaking requiring collaboration among various stakeholders. Data scientists and engineers are responsible for carefully curating and preprocessing training data to minimise biases. Additionally, robust evaluation techniques should be employed to identify and mitigate biases during algorithm development.

Transparency and explainability are also vital in addressing bias, and they should be core considerations when developing AI algorithms, ensuring they can withstand scrutiny and be subject to audibility. This can help identify and rectify biases in the algorithms, ensuring their fairness and accountability.

Furthermore, incorporating diverse perspectives and experiences in developing and evaluating AI algorithms can help mitigate bias. Including individuals from different backgrounds and ensuring diverse representation can lead to more comprehensive and fair algorithms.

Bias and fairness in AI algorithms are critical issues that require proactive attention. As AI continues to shape various aspects of our lives, it is imperative to ensure that these algorithms are free from biases perpetuating discrimination and inequality. By adopting transparent and inclusive practices, we can strive towards developing AI algorithms that promote fairness and equality for all.

Transparency, accountability, and regulation in AI have become increasingly vital as artificial intelligence technologies advance. With AI systems' rapid growth and integration in various aspects of our lives, ensuring these technologies are developed and deployed responsibly is crucial.

Transparency in AI pertains to the openness and clarity of AI systems and their decision-making processes. It involves comprehending how AI models are trained, what data is used, and how the algorithms make predictions or decisions. Transparent AI systems enable users and stakeholders to understand the technology better and foster trust.

Accountability is another fundamental aspect of AI. It entails attributing responsibility for the actions and decisions made by AI systems. In cases where AI systems are employed in critical applications such as healthcare or autonomous vehicles, accountability becomes even more crucial. Clear lines of responsibility and mechanisms for addressing errors or biases in AI systems are necessary to ensure accountability.

Regulation plays a vital role in governing AI technologies. As AI becomes more pervasive, regulations are needed to safeguard individuals' rights, ensure fairness, and address potential ethical concerns. Rules can help prevent the misuse or abuse of AI systems, establish data privacy and security standards, and promote responsible AI development and deployment.

Efforts have been made in recent years to develop frameworks and guidelines for AI transparency, accountability, and regulation. Organisations like the European Union and the OECD have proposed principles and procedures to address these issues. However, the challenge lies in implementing these principles and ensuring compliance across different industries and jurisdictions.

Transparency, accountability, and regulation in AI are interconnected and mutually reinforcing. Transparent AI systems enable accountability, and regulations provide a framework to enforce transparency and accountability. Together, they create a foundation for responsible and trustworthy AI.

As AI continues to advance, it is essential to prioritise transparency, accountability, and regulation. These elements are crucial for building trust in AI systems, protecting individual rights, and addressing ethical concerns. By fostering transparency, establishing clear lines of accountability, and implementing effective regulations, we can ensure that AI technologies are developed and deployed responsibly and beneficially.

The impact on employment and workforce dynamics is crucial in today's rapidly changing world. As technology advances and industries evolve, the way we work and the jobs available are also transforming. This has positive and negative consequences affecting individuals, organisations, and society.

One significant impact is the automation of tasks and the adoption of artificial intelligence (AI) technologies. While this can increase efficiency and productivity, it raises concerns about job displacement. Routine and repetitive tasks are being automated, meaning specific jobs may become obsolete. However, this also creates new opportunities for workers to develop skills that require human expertise, such as creativity, critical thinking, and emotional intelligence.

Another aspect to consider is the gig economy and the rise of freelance and contract work. With the advent of digital platforms, individuals now have greater flexibility in choosing when and where to work. This can benefit those seeking a better work-life balance or pursuing multiple income streams. However, it also introduces challenges such as job insecurity, lack of benefits, and income volatility.

Furthermore, globalisation has had a significant impact on employment and workforce dynamics. Companies now have access to a global talent pool, and outsourcing has become increasingly common. This has led to the offshoring of jobs, particularly in the manufacturing and customer service sectors. On the other hand, it has also opened new opportunities for international collaboration and the expansion of businesses into new markets.

In addition to these changes, there is a growing recognition of the importance of diversity and inclusion in the workforce. Companies are realising the benefits of having a diverse workforce in innovation, creativity, and problem-solving. Efforts are being made to create more inclusive work environments and reduce barriers to entry for underrepresented groups. However, progress must be made in achieving true equality and breaking systemic obstacles.

The impact on employment and workforce dynamics also extends to the skills and education needed for the jobs of the future. As technology evolves, a growing demand for workers with digital literacy and technical skills is growing. Continuous learning and upskilling are becoming essential to remaining competitive in the job market. This highlights the importance of lifelong learning and the need for educational institutions to adapt their curricula to meet the changing needs of the workforce.

The impact on employment and workforce dynamics is multifaceted and complex. Technological advancements, globalisation, the gig economy, and the push for diversity and inclusion shape it. While there are challenges and disruptions, there are also opportunities for individuals and organisations to thrive in this evolving landscape. Adapting to these changes requires a proactive approach, focusing on continuous learning, flexibility, and embracing new technologies. By doing so, we can navigate the changing world of work and create a future that benefits everyone.

SEVEN

The Future

ARTIFICIAL INTELLIGENCE (AI) HAS WITNESSED rapid advancements in recent years, presenting exciting and intriguing possibilities for the future. Looking ahead, there are several key areas where AI is anticipated to make significant strides and revolutionise industries.

One critical area where AI is set to have a substantial impact is healthcare. AI can assist in disease diagnosis and treatment plan recommendations and even predict potential health risks through its ability to analyse vast amounts of data and identify patterns. This has the potential to enhance patient outcomes and reduce healthcare costs significantly.

In the transportation sector, AI is already making waves with the development of autonomous vehicles. As the technology continues to improve, we can expect to witness a surge in self-driving cars on the roads, leading to increased safety and efficiency. AI can also optimise traffic management systems, reducing congestion and enhancing overall transportation infrastructure.

Customer service is another field where AI is poised to transform industries. With the rise of chatbots and virtual assistants, businesses can provide round-the-clock support to their customers. These AI-powered solutions can handle routine inquiries, allowing human agents to focus on more complex and personalised interactions. This not only improves customer satisfaction but also increases operational efficiency for businesses.

The entertainment industry is also set to benefit significantly from AI advancements. AI algorithms can analyse user preferences and behaviours to offer personalised recommendations for movies, music, and other forms of entertainment. This enhances the user experience and helps content creators reach their target audience more effectively.

One of the significant challenges associated with AI advancements lies in ensuring ethical and responsible use. Addressing concerns such as privacy, bias, and accountability is crucial as AI becomes more integrated into our daily lives. Striking the right balance between innovation and ethical considerations will be vital to harnessing the full potential of AI while safeguarding the interests of individuals and society.

The future of AI is bright and full of possibilities. From healthcare to transportation, customer service to entertainment, AI is poised to revolutionise industries and improve our lives in countless ways. By embracing responsible development and addressing ethical concerns, we can unlock the true potential of AI and create a future where humans and intelligent machines coexist harmoniously.

AI plays a crucial role in space exploration and scientific research. With advancements in artificial intelligence technology, scientists and researchers can leverage its capabilities to enhance their understanding of the universe and make groundbreaking discoveries.

One of the key areas where AI is making a significant impact is in the analysis of large sets of astronomical data. Space telescopes and observatories capture massive amounts of data from distant galaxies, stars, and other celestial objects. Analysing this data manually would be a daunting task, if not impossible. However, with AI algorithms and machine learning techniques, scientists can process and analyse this data at an unprecedented scale and speed. This enables them to identify patterns, anomalies, and new phenomena that could have gone unnoticed.

AI is also instrumental in the autonomous exploration of celestial bodies. Robotic spacecraft with AI systems can make independent decisions and adapt to unexpected situations. This is particularly important in missions to planets, asteroids, and moons where real-time communication with Earth is not feasible. AI-powered rovers and landers can navigate treacherous terrains, collect samples, and perform experiments, all while making intelligent decisions based on their surroundings.

Moreover, AI is revolutionising scientific research by accelerating the process of hypothesis generation and experimentation. AI algorithms can analyse vast amounts of scientific literature, identify relevant information, and generate hypotheses that scientists can investigate further. This saves time and helps researchers uncover insights and connections that might have been overlooked.

In addition to these applications, AI is also used to simulate and model complex astronomical phenomena. By creating virtual environments and running simulations, scientists can better understand galaxy formation, stellar evolution, and planetary dynamics. This allows them to test hypotheses, refine theories, and gain deeper insights into the universe's workings.

However, it is essential to note that while AI is a powerful tool in space exploration and scientific research, it is not a substitute for human expertise. Scientists and researchers play a crucial role in designing, interpreting, and validating the results obtained from AI systems. Human intuition, creativity, and domain knowledge are still essential in making sense of the vast data and formulating meaningful scientific questions.

AI has revolutionised space exploration and scientific research by enabling faster and more efficient astronomical data analysis, facilitating the autonomous exploration of celestial bodies, accelerating hypothesis generation, and providing insights through simulations and modelling. As AI advances, it holds immense potential to unlock further discoveries and deepen our understanding of the universe.

AI and climate change mitigation

Climate change is one of the most pressing challenges of our time. The Earth's climate is rapidly changing due to human activities, resulting in rising temperatures, extreme weather events, and biodiversity loss. As the consequences of climate change become more apparent, there is an urgent need for practical solutions to mitigate its impact and ensure a sustainable future for our planet.

Artificial intelligence (AI) has emerged as a powerful tool for addressing climate change's complex and interconnected challenges. AI technologies, such as machine learning and data analytics, can revolutionise our approach to climate change mitigation by enabling us to make more informed decisions and take proactive actions.

One area where AI can significantly impact is energy management and efficiency. AI-powered algorithms can analyse vast amounts of data to identify patterns and optimise energy consumption. This can lead to more efficient energy use in various sectors, including transportation, manufacturing, and buildings. By reducing energy waste and improving efficiency, AI can help reduce greenhouse gas emissions and slow down the pace of global warming.

Another area where AI can contribute to climate change mitigation is developing renewable energy sources. AI algorithms can analyse weather patterns and other data to optimise deploying renewable energy systems like solar and wind power. This can help maximise energy production and minimise reliance on fossil fuels, reducing greenhouse gas emissions.

AI can also play a crucial role in climate change adaptation and resilience. By analysing climate data and predicting future climate scenarios, AI can help communities and policymakers better understand the risks and develop effective strategies to adapt to changing conditions. For example, AI can forecast the impacts of rising sea levels and identify areas at high risk of flooding, allowing for better planning and infrastructure development.

Furthermore, AI can facilitate the monitoring and managing of ecosystems and natural resources. AI-powered sensors and drones can collect real-time data on environmental indicators, such as air and water quality, biodiversity, and deforestation. This data can then be analysed to identify trends, detect anomalies, and inform conservation efforts. By providing accurate and timely information, AI can support the preservation and sustainable management of our natural resources.

However, it is essential to recognise that AI is not a silver bullet for climate change mitigation. It is just one tool in a broader set of strategies to address this global challenge. In addition to AI, we need policy changes, international cooperation, and individual actions to achieve meaningful and lasting results.

AI has the potential to revolutionise our approach to climate change mitigation. By harnessing the power of AI technologies, we can optimise energy use, accelerate the transition to renewable energy, enhance climate resilience, and protect our natural resources. However, using AI responsibly and ethically is essential, ensuring it benefits all stakeholders and does not exacerbate existing inequalities. With concerted efforts and the right approach, AI can be a valuable ally in the fight against climate change.

The potential for human-AI collaboration is vast and holds immense promise for various domains. As artificial intelligence continues to advance rapidly, there is increasing recognition of the benefits that can arise from humans and AI working together.

In healthcare, human-AI collaboration has the potential to revolutionise patient care. AI algorithms can analyse vast medical data, helping doctors make more accurate diagnoses and treatment plans. By leveraging the power of AI, healthcare professionals can access insights and recommendations that can save lives and improve outcomes.

In business, human-AI collaboration can lead to increased productivity and efficiency. AI-powered tools can automate repetitive tasks, allowing human workers to focus on more complex and strategic activities. With AI handling mundane tasks like data entry and analysis, employees can allocate their time and skills to areas that require creativity and critical thinking.

Education is another area where human-AI collaboration can bring significant benefits. AI-powered tutoring systems can provide personalised learning experiences, adapting to each student's needs and pace. By leveraging AI's capabilities in data analysis and natural language processing, educational platforms can offer tailored feedback and guidance, enhancing the learning process.

In the realm of creativity, human-AI collaboration can unlock new possibilities. AI algorithms can generate novel ideas and assist artists in their creative endeavours. Whether it's composing music, creating visual art, or writing literature, AI can serve as a collaborator, offering unique perspectives and pushing the boundaries of artistic expression.

However, it is essential to acknowledge the challenges and ethical considerations of human-AI collaboration. Ensuring transparency, accountability, and fairness in AI systems is crucial to avoiding biases and unintended consequences. Additionally, balancing human judgement and AI recommendations is essential to preserving human autonomy and decision-making.

To fully harness the potential of human-AI collaboration, interdisciplinary efforts are required. Experts from various fields, including AI researchers, ethicists, policymakers, and practitioners, must collaborate and develop frameworks that promote responsible and beneficial use of AI technologies.

The potential for human-AI collaboration is immense across multiple domains. By leveraging the strengths of both humans and AI, we can achieve remarkable advancements in healthcare, business, education, creativity, and beyond. However, it is vital to approach this collaboration with ethical considerations and interdisciplinary collaboration to ensure that AI serves as a tool to augment human capabilities.

EIGHT

Implementations and Strategies

ARTIFICIAL INTELLIGENCE (AI) HAS GAINED significant traction in both personal and professional environments, leading to a transformative impact on our lifestyles and work practices. From intelligent personal assistants to advanced analytics tools, AI has the potential to streamline processes, enhance decision-making capabilities, and foster innovation across various domains. If you are considering the adoption of AI in your personal or professional life, it is imperative to follow these key steps.

Develop a Comprehensive Understanding of AI:

Begin by acquiring a fundamental comprehension of the principles and functioning of AI. Familiarise yourself with machine learning, natural language processing, and neural networks. This knowledge will enable you to grasp AI's potential applications and limitations in diverse contexts.

AI is a rapidly evolving field with immense potential for revolutionising various industries and aspects of our daily lives. To navigate this dynamic domain successfully, it is essential to establish a strong foundation of knowledge on the fundamental aspects of AI.

At its core, AI refers to developing intelligent machines capable of performing tasks that typically require human intelligence. These tasks encompass speech recognition, decision-making, problem-solving, and visual perception. AI systems are designed to learn from data, adapt to new inputs, and enhance performance over time.

To embark on your journey to comprehend AI, it is crucial to familiarise yourself with key concepts such as machine learning, natural language processing, and neural networks. Machine learning, a subset of AI, focuses on enabling computers to learn from data without explicit programming. This technique empowers machines to enhance their performance on specific tasks through experience and iterative adjustments.

Another critical aspect of AI is natural language processing (NLP), which involves interactions between computers and human language. NLP enables machines to understand, interpret, and generate human language, forming the foundation for various applications like virtual assistants, chatbots, and language translation systems.

Neural networks, inspired by the structure and functioning of the human brain, play a pivotal role in AI systems. Comprising interconnected nodes, or "neurons," that process and transmit information, neural networks excel in tasks such as image recognition, speech recognition, and natural language processing.

A comprehensive understanding of AI and its underlying concepts will equip you with the ability to comprehend the potential applications and limitations of AI in different contexts. Moreover, it will enable you to make informed decisions when implementing AI solutions in your projects or organisations. Embark on the journey of comprehending AI by developing a fundamental knowledge of its basics. By familiarizing yourself with concepts such as machine learning, natural language processing, and neural networks, you will be equipped to navigate the potential and limitations of AI in diverse fields. So, delve into the realm of AI and unlock its transformative possibilities!

Identify suitable use cases.

Determine the specific personal or professional requirements where AI can deliver value. Whether it involves automating repetitive tasks, enhancing customer experiences, or optimising business operations, identifying suitable use cases is essential for prioritising and focusing AI adoption efforts.

AI has emerged as a powerful tool with the potential to revolutionise various aspects of our personal and professional lives. Its ability to process substantial amounts of data and make informed decisions empowers it to enhance efficiency, improve customer experiences, and drive innovation across industries. However, to fully leverage the power of AI, it is crucial to identify use cases that align with your specific needs and goals.

The initial step in effectively harnessing AI involves identifying areas where it can add value. This necessitates thoroughly analysing your personal or professional requirements and determining how AI can address them. For instance, if you spend significant time on repetitive tasks like data entry or report generation, AI can automate these processes, freeing time for more strategic activities.

Similarly, many businesses prioritise enhancing customer experiences. AI can analyse customer data, identify patterns and trends, and provide personalised recommendations or solutions. By understanding customer preferences and behaviours, businesses can tailor their offerings to meet individual needs, increasing customer satisfaction and loyalty.

Optimising business operations is another area where AI can have a substantial impact. From supply chain management to inventory optimisation, AI algorithms can process vast amounts of data and make real-time decisions to streamline operations and reduce costs. By automating routine tasks and providing valuable insights, AI can assist businesses in making informed decisions and staying ahead of the competition.

Once potential use cases have been identified, it is pivotal to prioritise and focus AI adoption efforts. Not all use cases will have the same impact or feasibility within your context. By understanding your goals and constraints, you can determine which use cases should be given priority and allocate resources accordingly. This approach ensures that your AI initiatives deliver maximum value and impact.

Identifying suitable use cases is critical in leveraging AI for personal or professional needs. Whether it involves automating tasks, enhancing customer experiences, or optimising business operations, recognising the areas where AI can provide value is essential for successful AI adoption.

Staying updated on the latest research and advancements in artificial intelligence is paramount. Fake intelligence conferences, workshops, and online communities offer valuable opportunities for learning from experts, exchanging knowledge, and staying informed about cutting-edge techniques and trends. By remaining informed, organisations can adapt their artificial intelligence strategies and capitalise on emerging technologies.

To fully harness the power of artificial intelligence, organisations must prioritise acquiring resources and tools necessary for implementation. This involves investing in data, computing power, frameworks, expertise, and development platforms. By staying informed about the latest research and trends, organisations can pave the way for successful artificial intelligence initiatives, unlocking new possibilities for innovation and driving growth.

Developing artificial intelligence talent and expertise is critical to fostering innovation and maintaining competitiveness in today's rapidly evolving technological landscape. As artificial intelligence continues to reshape industries and revolutionise how we live and work, organisations recognise the necessity of investing in artificial intelligence capabilities.

Attracting and hiring individuals with the necessary skills and knowledge is critical in cultivating artificial intelligence talent. This often involves actively seeking professionals who deeply understand artificial intelligence concepts, algorithms, and methodologies. Additionally, organisations must foster a culture encouraging continuous learning and professional development in artificial intelligence. This can be achieved through training programmes, workshops, and collaborations with academic institutions.

Once the appropriate talent is onboard, organisations must provide opportunities for these individuals to apply their skills and contribute to artificial intelligence projects. This can include assigning them to cross-functional teams, where they can collaborate with experts from different disciplines and gain valuable insights from diverse perspectives. Additionally, organisations should create an environment encouraging experimentation and risk-taking, allowing artificial intelligence talent to explore innovative approaches and push boundaries.

Investing in research and development is another crucial aspect of building artificial intelligence expertise. This involves allocating resources to explore new artificial intelligence techniques, algorithms, and applications. By staying at the forefront of artificial intelligence research, organisations can identify emerging trends and technologies and leverage them to gain a competitive edge. Active participation in fake intelligence conferences, workshops, and forums, where experts share their knowledge and experiences, fosters collaboration and learning.

Collaboration with external partners, such as universities, research institutions, and startups, can also be vital in building artificial intelligence expertise. Organisations can tap into a broader talent pool, access cutting-edge research, and leverage shared resources by establishing partnerships. Collaborations can take various forms, from joint research projects to mentorship programmes, providing valuable opportunities for knowledge exchange and skill development.

In addition to acquiring and cultivating artificial intelligence (AI) expertise, organisations should prioritise cultivating a nurturing and inclusive AI environment. This entails the promotion of diversity and inclusivity, recognising that diverse perspectives and experiences contribute to developing robust and ethically sound AI solutions. It also necessitates establishing a transparent, accountable, and responsible AI framework wherein ethical considerations are integrated throughout the entirety of the AI development and implementation process. Organisations should institute clear guidelines and frameworks to ensure the ethical deployment of AI technology.

Pursuing AI proficiency is an ongoing endeavour that necessitates continual investment and adaptability. As technology advances and fresh challenges and opportunities arise, organisations must exhibit agility and embrace lifelong learning. By fostering a culture of curiosity, collaboration, and innovation, organisations can fully harness the potential of AI and generate significant impact within their respective industries.

Cultivating AI talent is indispensable for organisations to thrive in today's technology-driven world. Organisations can position themselves at the vanguard of AI innovation by attracting and nurturing the appropriate talent, investing in research, and enabling them to maintain competitiveness and a productive culture. This not only allows them to maintain competitiveness but also empowers them to effect positive and transformative change in society.

AI implementation requires expertise in machine learning and data science. Organisations should invest in building a skilled AI team comprising data scientists, machine learning engineers, and domain experts. These professionals can effectively develop, deploy, and maintain AI solutions, ensuring optimal performance and continuous improvement.

Organisations can leverage AI development platforms and integrated development environments (IDEs) to facilitate AI implementation. These platforms provide a unified data preprocessing, model development, and deployment environment. They often come with built-in AI tools, libraries, and visualisation capabilities, simplifying AI development.

Lastly, staying updated with the latest research and advancements in AI is crucial. AI conferences, workshops, and online communities offer opportunities to learn from experts, share knowledge, and stay informed about cutting-edge techniques and trends. Organisations can adapt their AI strategies and use emerging technologies by keeping up with the latest developments.

To fully leverage the power of artificial intelligence, organisations must prioritise acquiring resources and tools for AI implementation. This entails investing in data, computing power, frameworks, expertise, and development platforms. By staying abreast of the latest research and trends, organisations can pave the way for successful AI initiatives, unlocking new possibilities for innovation and driving growth.

Building AI talent and expertise is crucial to driving innovation and staying competitive in today's rapidly evolving technological landscape. As artificial intelligence continues to reshape industries and revolutionise how we live and work, organisations recognise the need to invest in developing AI capabilities.

One of the critical steps in building AI talent is attracting and hiring individuals with the right skills and knowledge. This often involves actively seeking professionals who deeply understand AI concepts, algorithms, and methodologies. Additionally, organisations must foster and encourage continuous learning and professional development in AI. This can be achieved through training programmes, workshops, and collaborations with academic institutions.

Once the right talent is onboard, organisations must provide opportunities for these individuals to apply their skills and contribute to AI projects. This can involve assigning them to cross-functional teams, where they can collaborate with experts from different disciplines and gain valuable insights from diverse perspectives. Furthermore, organisations should create an environment that encourages experimentation and risk-taking, allowing AI talent to explore innovative approaches and push boundaries.

Another crucial aspect of building AI expertise is investing in research and development. This involves allocating resources to explore new AI techniques, algorithms, and applications. By staying at the forefront of AI research, organisations can identify emerging trends and technologies and leverage them to create competitive advantages. This also includes actively participating in AI conferences, workshops, and forums, where experts share their knowledge and experiences, fostering collaboration and learning.

Collaboration with external partners, such as universities, research institutions, and startups, can also be vital in building AI expertise. Organisations can tap into a broader talent pool, access cutting-edge research, and leverage shared resources by establishing partnerships. Collaborations can take various forms, from joint research projects to mentorship programmes, providing valuable opportunities for knowledge exchange and skill development.

In addition to attracting and developing AI talent, organisations should also focus on creating a supportive and inclusive AI culture. This involves promoting diversity and inclusion, as different perspectives and experiences can lead to more robust and ethical AI solutions. It also requires fostering an environment that values transparency, accountability, and responsible AI practices. Organisations should establish clear guidelines and frameworks for AI development and deployment, ensuring that ethical considerations are embedded throughout the process.

AI expertise is an ongoing journey that requires continuous investment and adaptation. As technology evolves and new challenges and opportunities arise, organisations must stay agile and embrace lifelong learning. By nurturing a culture of curiosity, collaboration, and innovation, organisations can harness the full potential of AI and drive meaningful impact in their respective industries.

Building AI talent is essential for organisations to thrive in today's technology-driven world. Organisations can position themselves at the forefront of AI innovation by attracting and developing talent, investing in resources that enable them to stay competitive, and creating a supportive culture. This not only allows them to remain competitive but also empowers them to make a positive and transformative impact on society.

NINE

Real-life success stories

CASE STUDIES SERVE AS AN INDISPENSABLE resource for gaining insight into the effective utilisation of artificial intelligence (AI) by individuals and organisations. By examining real-world examples, we can learn about the strategies, technologies, and outcomes that drive success in this rapidly evolving field.

One case study involves a retail company implementing AI-powered demand forecasting to optimise inventory management. The company successfully predicted customer demand and adjusted inventory levels accordingly by analysing historical sales data, market trends, and external factors such as weather patterns. This resulted in substantial cost savings by minimising overstock and reducing out-of-stock situations, enhancing customer satisfaction and increasing sales.

Another compelling case study comes from the healthcare industry, where AI has been leveraged to enhance diagnostic accuracy and treatment effectiveness. For instance, a medical imaging company developed an AI algorithm capable of analysing medical scans and accurately detecting early signs of cancer. By harnessing AI's capacity to process vast amounts of data and identify subtle patterns, doctors were able to make more precise diagnoses and initiate timely interventions, ultimately saving lives.

In the financial sector, AI has revolutionised fraud detection and prevention. A significant bank implemented AI algorithms that analyse customer transaction data in real-time, effectively flagging suspicious activities and potentially fraudulent transactions. By automating this process, the bank significantly reduced false positives and improved the efficiency of its fraud detection system, resulting in time and resource savings while safeguarding customers' financial assets.

These examples exemplify how AI is effectively harnessed across diverse industries. The key takeaway from these case studies is that successful AI implementation necessitates a profound understanding of specific business needs, meticulous selection and customisation of AI technologies, and seamless integration into existing workflows. It is not a one-size-fits-all solution but rather a powerful tool that can drive substantial improvements in productivity, efficiency, and innovation when wielded correctly.

Case studies provide invaluable insights into the effective utilisation of AI in various contexts. By scrutinising real-world examples, we can learn from the successes and challenges others encounter, enabling us to make informed decisions and harness the full potential of AI in our endeavours.

Inspiring Examples of AI-Driven Innovations

Artificial intelligence (AI) has revolutionised various industries through its innovative applications. From healthcare to finance, AI-driven solutions transform how we live and work. In this article, we will explore some inspiring examples of AI-driven innovations that significantly impact different sectors.

1. Healthcare: AI is revolutionising healthcare by enabling the early detection and diagnosis of diseases. For instance, AI-powered algorithms can analyse medical images and identify abnormalities with high accuracy. This technology has the potential to improve patient outcomes and save lives.

2. Finance: AI is reshaping the financial industry by automating processes and enhancing decision-making. Machine-learning algorithms can analyse vast amounts of financial data to identify patterns and make predictions. This helps financial institutions with fraud detection, risk assessment, and investment management.

3. Transportation: AI plays a crucial role in developing autonomous vehicles. Self-driving cars with AI technology can navigate roads, avoid obstacles, and make real-time decisions. This has the potential to reduce accidents and improve overall transportation efficiency.

4. Manufacturing: AI-powered robots are transforming the manufacturing industry by increasing productivity and efficiency. These robots can precisely perform repetitive and complex tasks, reducing human errors and improving production speed. AI algorithms also enable predictive maintenance, minimising downtime, and optimising operations.

5. Retail: AI is revolutionising the retail industry with personalised customer experiences and improved supply chain management. Chatbots powered by AI can provide instant customer support, enhancing customer satisfaction. AI algorithms also analyse customer data to offer personalised product recommendations, increasing sales.

6. Education: AI is transforming education by enabling personalised learning experiences. AI-powered tutoring systems can adapt to individual students' needs and provide tailored instruction. Additionally, AI algorithms can analyse student performance data to identify areas of improvement and provide targeted interventions.

7. Agriculture: AI-driven innovations improve agricultural practices and increase crop yields. AI-powered drones equipped with sensors can monitor crop health and detect diseases or nutrient deficiencies. This allows farmers to take timely actions, optimising crop production and reducing waste.

These are just a few examples of AI driving innovation across various industries. As technology advances, we can expect even more exciting AI-driven solutions that will shape the future of our world.

AI-driven innovations are transforming industries and unlocking new possibilities. From healthcare to finance to transportation to education, AI is revolutionising how we live and work. By harnessing the power of AI, we can create a brighter and more efficient future for all.

Lessons learned and best practices provide invaluable insights derived from experience and observation. They serve as guiding principles for individuals and organisations, aiding in avoiding pitfalls and achieving success. This article will explore the significance of lessons learned and best practices, exploring their applicability in various contexts.

Let us define what we mean by "lessons learned." Lessons learned refer to the knowledge and understanding acquired through specific experiences, whether they result in success or failure. These lessons offer valuable insights into what worked well and what did not, enabling us to make informed decisions and improve our future endeavours.

Similarly, best practices are proven techniques or methods that consistently yield positive results. These practices have been refined over time and have demonstrated their efficacy in achieving desired outcomes. By adopting best practices, individuals and organisations can save time, resources, and effort by leveraging the experiences and wisdom of others.

So, why are lessons learned and best practices so important? Firstly, they allow us to build upon the knowledge and experiences of others. Instead of starting from scratch, we can learn from the successes and failures of those who have preceded us. This enables us to avoid common pitfalls and make better-informed decisions.

Secondly, lessons learned and best practices promote efficiency and effectiveness. Adhering to established guidelines and proven methods can streamline processes and achieve desired outcomes more efficiently. This saves time and resources and increases the likelihood of success.

Furthermore, lessons learned and best practices foster a culture of continuous improvement. By constantly seeking to learn from our experiences and the experiences of others, we can continuously refine our approaches and strive for excellence. This constant improvement mindset drives innovation and growth, allowing us to stay ahead in a rapidly evolving world.

Lessons we have learned and best practices are invaluable tools for personal and professional development. By embracing these principles, we can avoid common mistakes, achieve better results, and foster a culture of continuous improvement. So, let us assume the power of lessons and best practices and unlock our full potential.

TEN

The road ahead

This comprehensive summary will delve into the key insights and takeaways derived from our recent experience. We have acquired invaluable knowledge and perspectives throughout our journey that will undoubtedly shape our future endeavours. Let us explore the significant highlights and lessons learned in detail.

First and foremost, one of the most notable takeaways from this experience is the paramount importance of perseverance and determination. Despite encountering numerous challenges and obstacles, our unwavering commitment and focus allowed us to overcome them and achieve our goals. This experience has taught us that we can accomplish anything with the right mindset and determination.

Another crucial lesson learned from this journey is the power of collaboration and teamwork. We have realised that working together towards a common goal fosters creativity and innovation and facilitates the sharing of diverse perspectives and ideas. Through effective collaboration, we could harness each team member's strengths and expertise, resulting in exceptional outcomes.

Furthermore, this experience has underscored the significance of adaptability and flexibility. We quickly recognised that the landscape was constantly evolving, and to stay ahead, we had to be agile and adaptable. Embracing change and being open to new ideas and approaches proved instrumental in our success.

In addition, the critical factors for achieving success were identified as effective communication and active listening. The team members' ability to communicate clearly and concisely ensured everyone was aligned and working towards the same goals. Furthermore, active listening was crucial in promoting understanding and appreciation of different viewpoints, leading to more effective decision-making and problem-solving.

Throughout this journey, the importance of continuous learning and improvement was recognised. Opportunities to expand knowledge and skills were actively pursued through training programmes, workshops, and mentorship. By embracing a lifelong learning mindset, staying ahead of the curve and remaining competitive in their respective fields became possible.

Lastly, this experience emphasised the significance of celebrating milestones and acknowledging achievements.

Recognising team members' hard work and dedication boosts morale and fosters a positive and supportive work environment.

This summary highlights the key insights and takeaways from our recent experience. Lessons learned, from perseverance and collaboration to adaptability and continuous learning, have contributed to our growth and development. Reflecting on this journey, we are excited to apply these insights to future endeavours and continue striving for excellence.

Encouraging individuals to embrace the vast opportunities artificial intelligence (AI) presents is of utmost importance in today's rapidly evolving world. AI can potentially revolutionise various industries, including healthcare and finance, with far-reaching impact.

In recent years, AI has made significant advancements, enabling machines to perform tasks that were once exclusive to human capabilities. Speech recognition and image classification are just a few examples of AI's potential to enhance human abilities and improve efficiency. Leveraging the power of AI allows businesses and individuals to unlock new possibilities and achieve unprecedented levels of productivity.

One of the critical advantages of AI is its ability to process and analyse massive amounts of data in real-time. This empowers businesses to gain valuable insights and make data-driven decisions. AI-powered algorithms can identify patterns, trends, and correlations within data sets that would be nearly impossible for humans to detect. This opens new avenues for innovation and problem-solving, ultimately leading to improved outcomes and increased competitiveness.

Furthermore, AI has the potential to automate repetitive and mundane tasks, freeing up human resources to focus on more strategic and creative endeavours. Organisations can streamline operations, reduce costs, and improve efficiency by delegating routine tasks to AI systems. This allows employees to redirect their time and energy towards higher-value activities that require critical thinking and problem-solving. Addressing the ethical implications surrounding its use is crucial. As AI algorithms become more sophisticated, questions arise regarding privacy, bias, and accountability. Establishing robust frameworks and guidelines is essential to ensuring AI technologies' responsible and ethical deployment. By promoting transparency and accountability, we can maximise the benefits of AI while mitigating potential risks.

Encouraging individuals to embrace AI opportunities requires fostering education and awareness. By demystifying AI and showcasing its practical applications, we can dispel misconceptions and inspire individuals to explore its potential. Educational programmes and initiatives significantly equip individuals with the necessary skills to thrive in an AI-driven world. By nurturing a culture of continuous learning and adaptation, we empower individuals and organisations to leverage the full potential of AI.

Embracing AI opportunities is not merely a choice but a necessity in today's digital age. AI has the potential to transform industries, drive innovation, and improve the quality of life for individuals worldwide. By understanding its capabilities, addressing ethical concerns, and fostering education, we can create a future where AI is harnessed for the benefit of all. Let us embrace AI and embark on a journey of limitless possibilities.

Final thoughts on the future of AI and its potential impact

Artificial intelligence (AI) is rapidly evolving and has the potential to revolutionise various aspects of our lives. AI has already begun reshaping industries and enhancing efficiency in healthcare and transportation. Looking towards the future, there are several key areas where AI is expected to have a significant impact.

One promising area is healthcare, where AI-powered technologies can analyse vast amounts of medical data, leading to more accurate diagnoses and personalised treatment plans. Additionally, AI algorithms can aid in drug discovery, accelerating the development of new medications and improving patient outcomes.

Another domain poised for transformative impact is transportation. With the emergence of autonomous vehicles, AI can enhance road safety, reduce traffic congestion, and provide mobility solutions for individuals with limited mobility. Moreover, AI-powered logistics and supply chain management systems can optimise routes, improve efficiency, and reduce environmental impact.

Education is yet another field that can benefit from AI. Intelligent tutoring systems can provide personalised learning experiences, adapting to each student's needs and improving educational outcomes. AI can also assist in automating administrative tasks, enabling teachers to focus more on student engagement and individualised instruction.

However, as AI continues to advance, ethical considerations become paramount. Data privacy, algorithmic bias, and job displacement need proactive addressing. Striking the right balance between technological progress and human well-being is crucial to ensuring that AI benefits society.

The future of AI is bursting with boundless potential. Its unmatched ability to analyse vast amounts of data empowers us to revolutionise numerous domains, elevating our quality of life in extraordinary ways.

Imagine a healthcare landscape where AI seamlessly assists in diagnosing diseases and tailors personalised treatment plans, ensuring accurate and timely care. Imagine a transportation network where AI optimises traffic flow and safeguards us through autonomous vehicles, enhancing efficiency and safety. Imagine an educational realm where AI personalises learning experiences, providing tailored experiences that cater to individual needs and preferences, revolutionising how we acquire knowledge and skills. Visualise a future where AI seamlessly integrates into our daily lives, empowering us to make informed decisions, solve complex problems, and achieve new levels of productivity and innovation. Embrace the possibilities of a world where AI is not just a tool but a trusted companion, transforming industries and shaping a brighter future for all.

ELEVEN

Uncensored Artificial Intelligence and Dark GPT

ARTIFICIAL INTELLIGENCE, MUCH LIKE HUMANS, is influenced by its learning experiences. Exposure to harmful or biased information can lead to a 'Dark GPT,' which refers to an AI system trained on questionable data, resulting in offensive, unethical, or otherwise detrimental outputs. In the following section, we will delve into uncensored AI, explore its inherent dangers, and emphasise the critical importance of responsible AI training.

Uncensored AI refers to the idea of allowing AI systems to learn from unfiltered and unmoderated data without ethical or moral constraints. While this concept may initially appear appealing from a freedom of speech standpoint, it poses significant risks and challenges. One of the primary concerns with uncensored AI is the potential for perpetuating harmful biases and disseminating misinformation. When AI systems are trained on unfiltered data, they can absorb and amplify existing prejudices, stereotypes, and discriminatory patterns present in the data. This can lead to biased or discriminatory outputs, further entrenching societal inequalities.

Another issue with uncensored AI is the risk of spreading misinformation or fake news. AI models trained on unverified or unreliable sources may generate factually incorrect or misleading outputs. This can have serious consequences, as misinformation can quickly propagate and negatively impact public opinion, decision-making processes, and even democratic systems.

Furthermore, uncensored AI can also give rise to the production of offensive, harmful, or inappropriate AI-generated content. AI systems can generate outputs without proper ethical guidelines and moderation, including hate speech, explicit material, or other destructive behaviour. This can have severe societal implications, including the promotion of violence, harassment, or discrimination.

Responsible AI training becomes crucial to address these perils. AI developers and researchers must prioritise ethical considerations and ensure that AI systems are trained on diverse, balanced, and reliable data sources. Implementing robust moderation mechanisms and guidelines can help prevent the propagation of biases, misinformation, and harmful content. Additionally, involving diverse perspectives and interdisciplinary collaboration in AI development can help identify and mitigate potential ethical risks. This includes engaging ethics, sociology, psychology, and law experts to provide insights and guidance throughout AI development.

While uncensored AI may initially seem attractive, it carries significant risks and challenges. Responsible AI training, which encompasses ethical considerations, data moderation, and diverse perspectives, is essential to ensure that AI systems contribute positively to society without perpetuating biases, spreading misinformation, or generating harmful content. With the rapid advancement of AI technology, it becomes increasingly imperative to address the potential risks associated with its unregulated development. While AI can revolutionise various aspects of our lives, ensuring that its training is firmly rooted in ethical principles and responsible practices is of utmost importance.

The concept of uncensored AI raises a multitude of concerns. When an AI model is trained on unfiltered or biased data, it has the potential to perpetuate and amplify existing societal biases. This can manifest in various ways, from reinforcing stereotypes to endorsing discriminatory practices. The consequences of such outputs can be far-reaching, impacting individuals and entire communities.

One of the primary challenges in AI training lies in the accessibility and quality of training data. AI systems are typically trained on vast volumes of data, which can originate from diverse sources and may contain inherent biases. If these biases are not meticulously identified and mitigated, AI models can inherit and perpetuate those biases, leading to biased outputs and potentially harmful consequences.

The hazards of uncensored AI are not limited solely to biased outputs. Dark GPTs can also generate intentionally defamatory, offensive, or unethical content. Such outputs can have profound implications, from disseminating misinformation to inciting hatred or violence. Addressing these risks and establishing safeguards to prevent the development and deployment of AI systems that can potentially cause harm is imperative.

One of the critical challenges in addressing the hazards of uncensored AI is detecting and mitigating harmful outputs. Dark GPTs, in particular, can learn and replicate destructive patterns from the vast amount of data they are trained on. This poses a severe threat, as they can produce content that promotes discrimination, spreads propaganda, or even encourages illegal activities. To tackle this issue, it is crucial to implement robust content moderation mechanisms to identify and filter out harmful output. This requires a combination of advanced algorithms, human oversight, and clear guidelines to ensure that AI systems adhere to ethical standards. Additionally, continuous monitoring and evaluation of AI models can help identify and rectify any biases or harmful tendencies.

It is important to establish legal and ethical frameworks to hold developers and deployers of AI systems accountable for the potential harm caused by their creations. This includes setting up regulations and guidelines for developing, deploying, and using AI technologies. It is essential to involve diverse stakeholders, including experts from various fields, policymakers, and the public, in shaping these frameworks to ensure transparency, inclusivity, and fairness.

The hazards of uncensored AI extend beyond biased outputs and can encompass intentionally harmful, offensive, or unethical content. It is crucial to address these risks by implementing robust content moderation mechanisms, establishing legal and ethical frameworks, and involving diverse stakeholders in shaping AI policies. By doing so, we can prevent the development and deployment of AI systems that have the potential to cause harm and ensure that AI technology is used responsibly for the benefit of society.

Responsible AI training plays a pivotal role in mitigating these risks and ensuring the development of AI systems that align with societal values. This entails carefully curating and filtering training data and integrating ethical considerations into the design and development process. It involves establishing guidelines for acceptable and responsible AI behaviour and conducting regular audits and evaluations to ensure adherence to these principles.

The concept of uncensored AI raises significant concerns regarding the potential harm that can result from the uncontrolled development of AI systems. The risks associated with biased or harmful outputs necessitate a proactive approach to responsible AI training. By addressing these risks and prioritising ethical considerations, we can strive to develop AI systems that positively impact society while minimising potential harm.

To achieve responsible AI training, having a diverse and inclusive team of experts who can identify and address potential biases and ethical concerns is essential. This team should include individuals from various backgrounds, including ethicists, social scientists, and domain experts, who can provide different perspectives and ensure a comprehensive evaluation of AI systems. Additionally, transparency and explainability are crucial aspects of responsible AI training. Users should have access to information about how AI systems are trained, what data is used, and how decisions are made. This helps build trust with users and users but also allows for accountability and the identification of potential biases or errors.

Regular monitoring and evaluation of AI systems are essential to ensuring ongoing compliance with ethical guidelines. This can involve conducting audits of the training data, evaluating the performance of the AI system, and soliciting feedback from users and stakeholders. We can minimise potential risks and maximise their benefits by continuously assessing and improving AI systems.

Responsible AI training also involves considering the potential impact of AI systems on different stakeholders, including marginalised communities. It is essential to ensure that AI systems do not perpetuate or amplify existing inequalities but contribute to a more equitable and inclusive society.

In conclusion, responsible AI training is crucial for developing AI systems that align with societal values and minimise potential harm. By integrating ethical considerations, fostering transparency and accountability, and prioritising the well-being of all stakeholders, we can harness the power of AI for positive social impact.

TWELVE

The Future of Work

THE EMERGENCE OF ARTIFICIAL INTELLIGENCE (AI) has given rise to concerns regarding job displacement. However, implementing AI technology does not imply the obsolescence of human workers. On the contrary, it presents a fresh array of opportunities for individuals to excel in their skills by training AI systems, leveraging their unique human experience and expertise. This chapter aims to debunk prevalent misconceptions about AI assuming control over the world and delve into the transformative impact of AI on the workforce. We will explore the potential for AI to generate new job roles and discuss how the workforce can adapt and thrive in a world driven by AI.

AI technology has experienced rapid advancement in recent years, revolutionising diverse industries and sectors. As AI becomes more deeply integrated into our lives, there is growing apprehension that it will completely replace human workers. However, this fear is unfounded. While AI can automate repetitive and mundane tasks, it cannot replicate the creativity, critical thinking, and emotional intelligence that humans possess.

Instead of rendering humans obsolete, AI has the potential to complement and enhance human capabilities. By automating routine tasks, AI allows individuals to concentrate on more intricate and strategic endeavours. This shift-like work necessitates a novel approach to skills development and training.

One of AI's primary opportunities is individuals' ability to train AI systems. By leveraging their expertise and experience, humans can educate AI algorithms to perform tasks more efficiently and accurately. This symbiotic relationship between humans and AI creates a powerful synergy wherein humans provide the context, intuition, and judgement that AI lacks.

AI can assist in identifying patterns, trends, and insights that may not be discernible to humans alone. This collaboration between humans and AI can result in innovative solutions and discoveries that would otherwise be unattainable. By augmenting human capabilities with AI, individuals can unlock their full potential and achieve greater productivity and efficiency.

While it is true that AI will eliminate specific jobs, it will also generate new ones. As AI technology progresses, novel roles will emerge that necessitate a profound understanding of AI systems and their integration into various industries. These roles may encompass AI trainers, data scientists, AI ethicists, and AI system designers. Additionally, there will be an increasing demand for individuals who can bridge the gap between AI technology and business strategy, ensuring the effective utilisation of AI to drive organisational growth and innovation.

Individuals must embrace lifelong learning and acquire new skills to adapt and thrive in a world driven by AI. The future workforce will require technical expertise, critical thinking, creativity, and adaptability. Continuous upskilling and reskilling will be imperative to remain relevant and competitive in the job market.

The rise of AI does not signify the termination of human work but rather a transformation of work itself. AI has the potential to revolutionise industries, create new opportunities, and enhance human capabilities. By embracing AI technology and continuously developing our skills, we can navigate the evolving landscape of the workforce and thrive in an AI-driven world. The future of work is not one without humans but rather a collaborative partnership between humans and AI.

Therefore, it is essential to approach the integration of AI in the workforce with ethical considerations and responsible training practices to ensure a positive future for all. We must strive towards a world where AI is a tool for human progress and empowerment rather than replacing human labour.

THIRTEEN

Monetizing

In the digital transformation era, AI technology advancement presents many opportunities for individuals to generate online revenue. This chapter unveils various strategies and methods individuals can use to monetise AI effectively. From establishing your AI-based enterprise to leveraging AI for investment strategies, we will guide you through comprehensive and innovative approaches to capitalising on this groundbreaking technology.

AI has emerged as a transformative force in the digital landscape, driving operational efficiency and fostering innovation across various online enterprises. Flourishing AI-based businesses offer diverse services, from AI-driven web design to AI-powered digital marketing. By venturing into the realm of AI-based entrepreneurship, individuals cater to the growing demand for AI services and establish a sustainable source of online income.

Another lucrative avenue for online income generation through AI lies in AI stock trading. AI-powered stock trading platforms provide real-time insights and analytics, empowering investors to make well-informed decisions. These platforms predict market trends by harnessing machine learning algorithms, maximising profitability. However, as with any investment endeavour, conducting thorough research and evaluation is crucial before proceeding.

Harnessing the power of AI in content creation and digital marketing can yield significant rewards. AI tools analyse user behaviour and preferences to generate personalised content, resulting in heightened engagement and conversion rates. Additionally, AI can automate the SEO process, facilitating higher rankings and increased visibility for your content, ultimately leading to enhanced revenue generation.

Developing and selling AI applications or offering consulting services can be a substantial income source for individuals possessing technical expertise. Companies consistently seek ways to integrate AI into their business models and rely on the guidance of AI professionals for successful implementation. By positioning yourself as an AI expert, you can provide valuable insights and solutions to businesses, earning a substantial income. Additionally, freelancing platforms and online marketplaces offer opportunities to showcase your AI skills and connect with potential clients seeking AI-related services.

Furthermore, AI can be monetised by creating and selling AI-generated products. From AI-generated artwork to AI-powered virtual assistants, the possibilities are limitless. By tapping into the creative potential of AI, individuals can generate income by selling these unique and innovative products.

AI can be utilised to optimise and streamline existing business processes, leading to cost savings and increased efficiency. Businesses can reduce labour costs and enhance productivity by implementing AI-driven automation systems. As an AI consultant or service provider, you can assist companies in identifying areas where AI can be integrated and help them achieve their operational goals while earning a lucrative income.

The monetisation of AI offers individuals a wide range of opportunities to generate online income. Whether through entrepreneurship, investment strategies, content creation, consulting services, or the creation and sale of AI-generated products, individuals can capitalise on the transformative power of AI and secure a sustainable source of income in the digital era.

Entrepreneurship in the field of AI is a promising avenue for generating online income. By identifying market gaps and developing innovative AI solutions, individuals can create their startups and offer their products or services to a global audience. With the increasing demand for AI-powered technologies, there is ample opportunity for entrepreneurs to carve out a niche and establish a successful business.

Investment strategies also play a crucial role in monetising AI. Investing in AI companies or funds can yield significant returns as the AI industry grows. By staying informed about the latest trends and advancements in AI, individuals can make informed investment decisions and benefit from the financial rewards.

Content creation is another avenue for generating income in the AI space. This can include writing articles, creating videos, or hosting podcasts educating others about AI-related topics. By building a following and monetising their content through advertising or sponsorships, individuals can turn their passion for AI into a profitable venture.

Consulting services are in high demand as organisations seek guidance on implementing AI strategies. Individuals with expertise in AI can offer their services as consultants, helping businesses leverage AI technologies to improve their operations, enhance customer experiences, and drive growth. Consulting can be done remotely, allowing individuals to work with clients worldwide and earn a lucrative income.

In addition, the opportunity to monetise one's AI skills is uniquely presented through the development and commercialisation of AI-generated products. This can include developing AI-powered software, applications, or even AI-generated artwork. By marketing and selling these products online, individuals can tap into a global market and generate a steady income stream.

The monetisation of AI offers many opportunities for individuals to generate online income. Whether through entrepreneurship, investment strategies, content creation, consulting services, or the creation and sale of AI-generated products, individuals can leverage the power of AI to secure a sustainable source of income in the digital era. With the right skills, knowledge, and determination, anyone can take advantage of the transformative potential of AI and thrive in the online economy.

The first step towards monetising AI is to acquire the necessary skills and knowledge. This can be done through online courses, certifications, or even self-study. Understanding the fundamentals of AI, machine learning, and data analysis is crucial to utilise AI for income generation effectively.

Entrepreneurship is one avenue that individuals can explore. With AI, entrepreneurs can develop innovative solutions, products, or services that cater to specific market needs. The possibilities are endless, whether it's creating AI-powered chatbots, virtual assistants, or personalised recommendation systems. Entrepreneurs can build successful businesses and generate revenue by identifying a niche and leveraging AI technology.

Investment strategies in AI-related companies and technologies can also be lucrative. As AI continues to evolve and expand, numerous investment opportunities exist in AI startups, AI-driven companies, and AI-focused funds. By investing in these ventures, individuals can participate in the growth of the AI industry and potentially earn substantial returns.

Content creation is another avenue for monetising AI. With AI tools and platforms, individuals can create engaging and personalised content at scale. This can include AI-generated articles, videos, or even social media posts. By leveraging AI to automate content creation, individuals can save time and resources while still producing high-quality content that attracts an audience and generates income through advertising or sponsorship deals.

Consulting services in AI can also be highly profitable. As businesses increasingly adopt AI technologies, there is a growing demand for AI consultants who can provide guidance and expertise. Whether it's helping companies implement AI solutions, optimise algorithms, or analyse data, AI consultants can offer valuable insights and services that can be monetised.

Lastly, individuals can explore the creation and sale of AI-generated products. This can include AI-generated artwork, music, or even fashion designs. With AI algorithms that can generate unique and creative outputs, individuals can tap into the growing market for AI-generated products and sell them online.

The monetisation of AI offers individuals a wide range of opportunities to generate online income. By developing the right skills, knowledge, and determination, anyone can leverage the power of AI and thrive in the digital economy.

The possibilities are endless, whether through entrepreneurship, investment strategies, content creation, consulting services, or the creation and sale of AI-generated products. It's an exciting time to explore the potential of AI and turn it into a sustainable source of income.

FOURTEEN

Examples of strategies

THE FOLLOWING TABLE (T1) PROVIDES A detailed overview of different strategies to monetise AI. It includes a description of each method, the potential income it can generate, and the skills required. Whether you are a beginner exploring how to profit from AI or an experienced professional seeking to maximise your earnings, this table provides a comprehensive guide to understanding the diverse opportunities available in the AI market.

Strategy	Description	Potential Income	Required Skills
AI-BASED BUSINESS	Start a business offering AI-powered services like web designing and digital marketing.	High, depending on the scale of the business and the demand for services.	Business acumen, understanding of AI, marketing skills.
AI STOCK TRADING	Use AI-powered platforms for stock trading that provide real-time insights and market trend predictions.	High, but risk associated as with any investment.	Understanding of stock markets, knowledge of AI in finance.
CONTENT CREATION AND DIGITAL MARKETING	Use AI tools for personalized content creation and SEO automation.	Medium to high, depending on user engagement and conversion rates.	Content creation, digital marketing, understanding of AI in content creation.
DEVELOPING AND SELLING AI APPLICATIONS	Develop AI applications to meet specific needs in various industries and sell them.	High, depending on the applicability and innovativeness of the application.	Technical skills in AI, understanding of specific industry needs.
AI CONSULTING SERVICES	Offer consulting services to companies seeking to integrate AI into their business models.	High, depending on the complexity of the project and the company's budget for AI integration.	Deep understanding of AI consulting skills, understanding of various industries.

T1

Disclaimer:

- *The information provided in the table above is for informational purposes only.*
- *The content generation methods, descriptions, monetisation opportunities, AI platforms, and mobile apps listed are based on general knowledge and industry trends.*
- *Users are advised to conduct their own research and due diligence before implementing any of the strategies mentioned or utilising the specified AI platforms and mobile apps.*
- *The monetisation opportunities mentioned may vary based on individual circumstances, market conditions, and other factors.*
- *Users should carefully evaluate their goals and requirements before making decisions related to content generation, monetisation, or adopting AI technologies.*

- *The creators of this table are not responsible for any loss, damages, or consequences resulting from the use of the information provided.*
- *Users engage with the content at their own risk and discretion.*

1. AI-Based Business

Example: AI-Powered Digital Marketing Agency

Steps:

Market Research:

- Identify the target market and industries where AI-powered digital marketing services are in demand.
- Analyse competitors and their offerings.

Business Plan:

- Develop a comprehensive business plan outlining your services, target audience, marketing strategy, and financial projections.
- Consider partnerships with AI developers or experts.

Skill Development:

- Acquire or enhance your skills in business management, AI technologies, and digital marketing.

- Consider hiring or collaborating with experts in areas where you lack proficiency.

Technology Infrastructure:

- Set up the necessary technology infrastructure to support AI-powered services.
- Invest in AI tools, platforms, and systems that align with your business goals.

Build a team:

- Assemble a team with various skills, including AI specialists, marketers, and business development professionals.

Client Acquisition:

- Implement a targeted marketing strategy to attract clients.
- Showcase case studies and success stories to demonstrate the effectiveness of your AI-powered solutions.

Service Delivery:

- Tailor AI solutions to meet the specific needs of clients.
- Provide ongoing support and optimisation to ensure the success of AI implementations.

Scaling:

- Monitor the performance of your business and identify opportunities for scaling.
- Explore partnerships and collaborations to expand your reach.

2. AI Stock Trading

Example: AI-Powered Stock Trading Platform

Steps:

Regulatory Compliance:

- Understand and comply with regulatory requirements related to AI-powered stock trading platforms.

Data Collection and Analysis:

- Implement algorithms for real-time data collection and analysis.
- Develop models for market trend predictions and risk assessment.

Platform Development:

- Build a user-friendly platform with features such as real-time market insights, portfolio management, and risk analysis.

Security Measures:

- Implement robust security measures to protect user data and financial transactions.

Testing:

- Conduct thorough testing of the AI algorithms to ensure accuracy and reliability.

User Education:

- Provide educational resources to users on using the platform and interpreting AI-generated insights.

Launch and Marketing:

- Launch the platform with a marketing campaign highlighting its unique features and benefits.
- Offer promotions or incentives to attract initial users.

Monitoring and Updates:

- Continuously monitor the performance of the AI algorithms.
- Provide regular updates and improvements based on user feedback and market changes.

3. Content Creation and Digital Marketing

Example: AI-enhanced content Creation Agency

Steps:

Identify Niche:

- Identify a niche where personalised content creation and SEO automation can significantly impact.

Tool Selection:

- Choose or develop AI tools that align with content creation needs, such as natural language processing for writing or image recognition for visual content.

Content Strategy:

- Develop a content strategy that integrates AI tools seamlessly.
- Focus on personalisation, relevance, and SEO optimisation.

Team Training:

- Train content creators and digital marketers on how to use AI tools effectively.
- Emphasise creativity in conjunction with AI capabilities.

Client Onboarding:

- Onboard clients by showcasing the benefits of AI-enhanced content creation, including improved engagement and conversion rates.

Performance Tracking:

- Implement analytics to track the performance of AI-generated content.
- Iterate and optimise based on data insights.

Client Communication:

- Maintain open communication with clients, providing regular updates on the performance of AI-driven content.

Industry Networking:

- Attend industry events and network with businesses looking for innovative content solutions.

4. Developing and Selling AI Applications

Example: AI-Based Healthcare Application

Steps:

Identify healthcare needs:

- Research and identify specific needs within the healthcare industry that can be addressed with AI applications.

Collaborate with experts:

- Collaborate with healthcare professionals and AI experts to understand the industry's nuances and potential solutions.

Prototyping:

- Develop prototypes of AI applications tailored to solve identified problems in healthcare.

Regulatory Compliance:

- Navigate and comply with healthcare industry regulations to ensure AI applications' legal and ethical use.

Testing and validation:

- Conduct extensive testing and validation of the AI applications in real-world healthcare settings.

Partnerships:

- Explore partnerships with healthcare institutions, clinics, or technology providers for application testing and integration.

User Training:

- Develop user-friendly interfaces and provide training resources for healthcare professionals using the AI applications.

Sales and Marketing:

- Develop a sales and marketing strategy to promote AI applications to healthcare organisations.
- Highlight the efficiency, accuracy, and cost-effectiveness of the solutions.

5. AI Consulting Services

Example: AI Integration Consulting Firm

Steps:

Industry Specialisation: Choose industries where AI integration is in high demand (e.g., finance, healthcare, manufacturing).

Expert Team Formation: Assemble a team of AI experts, consultants, and industry specialists.

Needs Assessment: Work closely with clients to assess their specific needs, challenges, and opportunities for AI integration.

Customised Solutions: Develop customised AI solutions based on each client's requirements.

ROI Analysis: Provide a thorough analysis of the return on investment (ROI) for clients adopting AI solutions.

Implementation Support: Offer hands-on support during the implementation phase to ensure a smooth integration of AI into existing business processes.

Training Programmes: Develop training programmes for client teams to enhance their understanding of AI and its applications in their industry.

Continuous Support: Provide ongoing support, monitoring, and optimisation services to ensure the long-term success of AI integration.

THE SECOND TABLE (T2) SUMMARISES VARIOUS AI-driven content generation techniques and the corresponding revenue generation prospects. Moreover, it lists AI platforms and their associated mobile applications, enabling an efficient exploration of these strategies.

DISCLAIMER:

- *The information provided in the table above is for informational purposes only.*
- *The content generation methods, descriptions, monetisation opportunities, AI platforms, and mobile apps listed are based on general knowledge and industry trends.*
- *Users are advised to conduct their research and due diligence before implementing the mentioned strategies or utilising the specified AI platforms and mobile apps.*
- *The monetisation opportunities mentioned may vary based on individual circumstances, market conditions, and other factors.*
- *Users should carefully evaluate their goals and requirements before making decisions related to content generation, monetisation, or adopting AI technologies.*
- *The creators of this table are not responsible for any loss, damages, or consequences resulting from the use of the information provided.*
- *Users engage with the content at their own risk and discretion.*

Glossary

Adversarial Machine Learning: A branch of machine learning focused on defending against adversarial attacks, where malicious actors attempt to manipulate or deceive AI systems by injecting carefully crafted input data.

AI ethics involves the study and implementation of moral principles and values in developing and utilising artificial intelligence systems. This encompasses fairness, transparency, accountability, privacy, and human rights considerations.

AI-powered assistants are computer programs that utilise AI technologies to perform tasks or answer inquiries on behalf of users. These assistants can range from simple virtual assistants like Siri or Alexa to more sophisticated business assistants.

Artificial General Intelligence (AGI) refers to an AI system capable of performing any intellectual task that a human can. AGI is often regarded as the next frontier in AI development.

Artificial neural networks, or deep learning models, are a subset of machine learning that employs interconnected nodes to process information. Like the human brain, these networks can acquire knowledge from data through iterative interactions with their environment.

Artificial Neural Network (ANN): A computational model inspired by the human brain's neural structure, consisting of interconnected nodes (neurons) that process and transmit information. ANNs are fundamental to deep learning.

Augmented Intelligence: A form of artificial intelligence that collaborates with humans to enhance their capabilities rather than replacing them entirely. This approach recognises the significance of human oversight and decision-making for complex tasks.

Chatbot: A computer program designed to engage in text- or voice-based conversations with users. Chatbots often use natural language processing (NLP) techniques to understand and respond to user queries.

Computer Vision: The field of AI enables machines to interpret and understand visual information from the world, such as images and videos. It has applications in image recognition, object detection, and facial recognition.

Conversational AI: AI systems designed to engage in natural language conversations with users. They are used in chatbots, virtual assistants, and customer service applications to interact with and conversationally assist users.

Diffusers are technologies that utilise algorithms to distribute resources, such as energy or data, efficiently. This can help mitigate the environmental impact of AI and promote sustainability.

Edge Computing: A computing paradigm where AI processing occurs locally on devices (at the network's „ edge „ rather than relying solely on centralised cloud servers. This reduces latency and enhances privacy in AI applications.

Ethical AI Design: Intentionally designing AI systems to adhere to ethical principles and values, including fairness, transparency, privacy, and accountability, to minimise biases and potential harm.

Explainable AI: Focuses on developing AI systems that provide clear and understandable explanations for their decisions and actions. This promotes trust, accountability, and the ethical use of AI.

Federated Learning: A decentralised machine learning approach where models are trained on distributed data sources without exchanging them centrally. It's often used in privacy-sensitive applications where data cannot be easily shared.

Generative Adversarial Networks (GANs) are neural network architectures used in unsupervised machine learning. GANs consist of two networks, a generator and a discriminator, that are trained adversarially. They are often used for tasks like image generation and style transfer.

Human-in-the-Loop (HITL): a machine learning or AI system involving human intervention or oversight in decision-making. HITL systems combine AI capabilities with human expertise to improve accuracy and trustworthiness.

Language Model (LLM): A computer program that learns language structure and context to generate text resembling human expression.

Machine Learning Engineer: A professional responsible for developing and deploying machine learning models, including data collection, model training, and application integration.

Natural Language Generation (NLG): A subfield of natural language processing (NLP) that focuses on generating human-like text or language. NLG systems can create reports, articles, or even chatbot responses.

Natural Language Processing (NLP) is a branch of AI that concentrates on understanding and processing human language. NLP finds applications in various domains, such as chatbots, voice assistants, and sentiment analysis.

Neural Architecture Search (NAS): An automated approach to designing optimal neural network architectures for specific tasks. NAS algorithms explore a search space of architectures to find the most efficient ones.

Neuroevolution: An approach to training artificial neural networks inspired by biological evolution. It involves evolving neural network architectures and parameters to improve performance on specific tasks.

Pre-training: Training a model on a comprehensive dataset to acquire general features and patterns before fine-tuning it for a specific task. This approach has improved performance and reduced training time in natural language processing tasks.

Quantum Machine Learning: The intersection of quantum computing and machine learning. Quantum computers have the potential to significantly speed up certain types of machine learning algorithms and solve complex optimisation problems.

Reinforcement Learning: A machine learning paradigm where agents learn to make decisions by interacting with an environment. They receive feedback through rewards or penalties, enabling them to learn optimal strategies over time.

Regularisation: A technique to prevent overfitting by introducing penalties or constraints to a model's parameters.

Robotic Process Automation (RPA): Involves using software robots or AI systems to automate repetitive tasks traditionally performed by humans. This enables human employees to focus on more intricate and creative work.

Search Engine Optimization (SEO): Optimising a website or web content to increase visibility and rank higher in search engine results pages. AI technologies are increasingly employed in SEO to analyse data and enhance website performance.

Self-Supervised Learning: A machine learning technique where models learn from unlabeled data or data labelled automatically without human annotation. It's a form of unsupervised learning that has shown promise in various AI tasks.

Sentiment Analysis: An NLP technique that determines the sentiment or emotional tone expressed in text, often used to gauge public opinion or customer feedback.

Supervised Learning: A machine learning paradigm where models are trained on labelled data to learn a mapping from inputs to desired outputs. It's widely used in tasks like classification and regression.

Swarm Intelligence: A branch of AI that takes inspiration from the collective behaviour of social insects, such as ants and bees. Algorithms in swarm intelligence simulate the interactions of individuals in a group to solve complex optimisation and decision-making problems.

Transfer Learning: A machine learning technique where a model trained on one task is leveraged as a starting point for training on a different but related task. It's often used to transfer knowledge from one domain to another, reducing the required training data.

Unsupervised Learning: A machine learning paradigm where models learn patterns and structure in data without explicit labels. Typical applications include clustering and dimensionality reduction.

Artificial Intelligence as a Service (AIaaS): A cloud computing offering that provides access to AI and machine learning capabilities through APIs (Application Programming Interfaces). This allows developers and businesses to leverage AI tools without building and training their own models.

About the Author

Elijah Carter, the author of "21st Century Revolution" based in London, is committed to integrating artificial intelligence into people's lives to simplify and innovate daily routines. His primary focus is making AI accessible and user-friendly, firmly believing in its potential to revolutionise various aspects of society positively. Carter's vision is driven by the notion that AI can enhance our lives and drive innovation.

In this book, Carter explores using AI to streamline tasks, enhance efficiency, and ultimately generate income. He emphasises that AI should not be perceived as a threat to human jobs but as a tool to boost productivity and create new opportunities. Carter's book delves into several industries where AI can significantly impact healthcare, finance, transportation, and customer service. Practical examples and case studies illustrate how AI can transform these sectors.

Ethical AI development is a key message conveyed in Carter's work. He advocates for responsible and transparent practices to ensure AI algorithms' fairness, impartiality, and accountability. Carter believes ethical considerations *should be at the forefront of AI implementation to prevent adverse consequences.*

Throughout his book, Carter encourages readers to embrace AI as a catalyst for progress and innovation. He offers insights on integrating AI into daily lives and provides practical advice on selecting suitable AI systems and understanding their limitations. "21st Century Revolution" serves as a guide to understanding AI's potential and a call to action. Carter urges readers to actively participate in shaping the future of AI, emphasising that everyone has a role in harnessing its benefits and mitigating its risks.

As a London-based author, Carter possesses extensive knowledge of the advancements and challenges of AI in a global context. His expertise and passion for the subject shine through in his writing, making "21st Century Revolution" an informative and thought-provoking read for anyone interested in the intersection of technology and society.